How to Build
PATHS, STEPS
& FOOTBRIDGES

How to Build
PATHS, STEPS
& FOOTBRIDGES

The Fundamentals of Planning, Designing, and Constructing
Creative Walkways in Your Home Landscape

PETER JESWALD

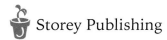 Storey Publishing

The mission of Storey Publishing is to serve our customers by publishing practical information that encourages personal independence in harmony with the environment.

Cover and text design by Kent Lew
Text production by Cindy McFarland, Jennifer Jepson Smith, and Vicky Vaughn
Cover photographs © Roger Foley, back cover; Blake Gardner, front cover, bottom right; © Janet Loughrey, front cover, left; © Maggie Oster, front cover, top right. See page 225 for complete photography credits.
Illustrations by Terry Dovaston and Associates
Indexed by Robert Swanson

The information in this book is true and complete to the best of our knowledge. All recommendations are made without guarantee on the part of the author or Storey Publishing. The author and publisher disclaim any liability in connection with the use of this information. For additional information please contact Storey Publishing, 210 MASS MoCA Way, North Adams, MA 01247.

Storey books are available for special premium and promotional uses and for customized editions. For further information, please call 1-800-793-9396.

Printed in the United States by Von Hoffmann Graphics
10 9 8 7 6 5 4 3 2 1

Library of Congress Cataloging-in-Publication Data

Jeswald, Peter.
　How to build paths, steps & footbridges : the fundamentals of planning, designing, and constructing creative walkways in your home landscape / Peter Jeswald.
　　p. cm.
　Includes index.
　ISBN-13: 978-1-58017-487-9; ISBN-10: 1-58017-487-6 (pbk. : alk. paper)
　ISBN-13: 978-1-58017-575-3; ISBN-10: 1-58017-575-9 (hardcover : alk. paper)
　1. Garden walks. I. Title.

TH4970.J47 2005
624—dc22

2004025044

To my mother-in-law, Rose Krakauer, whose generous spirit

and undying support touched the lives of many and

made so much possible for me

■   ■   ■

CONTENTS

It was our son's sixth birthday, and eight of his friends were gathered on our deck, squirming with anticipation. It would be a first for all of us: a birthday party on a forest island.

The long, narrow island formed by a fork in Pumpkin Hollow Brook had always been a special place for our family, and because it was the end of summer and water levels were low, we thought it would make the perfect spot for a birthday party. My wife, Phyllis, and I had everything carefully planned: games among the trees, hot dogs cooked over a campfire, and cake, ice cream, and song.

Our short trek to the island began hand in hand and single file. We led the children down our sloping lawn and along the worn path that snaked its way to the brook. There, we stopped at a limbless, fallen tree that spanned the water. Standing on stones in the stream, Phyllis and I helped the young adventurers across. It was at this point that our carefully crafted plans began to change. The log crossing, it turned out, was great fun, and the kids made it into a game, crossing, recrossing, and crossing again.

After we convinced the children to keep moving forward, we rounded them up at the campfire site and spelled out the agenda. Before we could say *kindling*, they were off gathering wood. One boy asked if he could take down a small dead sapling at the bank of the stream. The tree was rotten, so he made quick work of it, with one hitch: he pushed it in the direction of the stream and the tree fell across it. While contemplating his next move, he noticed that behind the tree water was beginning to pool near the shore. He seemed instantly to realize that he had the makings of a dam. He called the others, and soon they were dragging branches and brush to add to the dam. The busy beavers spanned the brook in no time, and the dam became a second irresistible path across

the water. Some sections were sturdier than others, so the new game became trying to cross without sinking and getting wet.

After a while, someone spied a fallen, 30-inch hemlock bridging the banks downstream. Scrambling up the steep east bank, the excited band made a beeline for the tree. The hemlock was spiked at regular intervals with branches that kept the trunk elevated several feet off the ground and formed a crude railing; this made crossing a snap. Our adventurers-cum-engineers crafted steps from boughs bent under the tree and used the other broken branches as a framework for walls. The children laid brush and hemlock boughs against them, creating an impressively fortified bridge.

Eventually, we reminded them about the cake and ice cream and shepherded them back to the campfire site. In the end, my wife and I could only smile, happy that our careful planning went so well.

■   ■   ■

The kids certainly got a charge that day. What was it that made it such a powerful experience for them? Was it the realization that they could exert some measure of control over their environment? Joyful ingenuity? Fun?

As the children discovered, paths, steps, and footbridges are all about journeys: they help us depart and they help us arrive. Some of my fondest childhood memories involve paths: paths through my grandmother's hayfields, along cliffs in abandoned stone quarries, through the woods under the sheltering boughs of majestic pines. Whether serendipitous or man-made, paths evoke a sense of wonder and adventure; they take us where we want to go and guide us to places we've never been.

■   ■   ■

Now more than ever, Americans are investing time and money to improve and personalize their homes. Additions, renovations, and other physical improvements account for much of that activity, but homeowners are also turning their attention outdoors, demonstrating renewed interest in gardening and landscaping. Flowers and vegetables gardens abound; trees, bushes, and shrubs transform ubiquitous lawns into lush landscapes; and decks, arbors, and dense plantings create outdoor "rooms" for entertaining and serene spaces for quiet contemplation.

Not surprisingly, ease of access to, and movement through, these outdoor spaces is an important part of their appeal. Paths, steps, and footbridges can play a dynamic role in organizing, articulating, and enlivening the exterior living environment. Such projects connect us to the earth and promote a sense of stewardship. They also provide a rare opportunity for us to express our creativity while producing outdoor features that serve a utilitarian purpose.

Having picked up this book, you're probably considering investing in one or more improvements to the yard or landscape around your home. Perhaps you have

- a specific project in mind: *how can I get from point A to point B?*
- a challenging situation that needs to be addressed: *how can I maximize the use of my yard and landscape, or reach areas of yard that are difficult to access?*
- a general goal you'd like to achieve: *can I build something that's practical and, at the same time, add some pizzazz to my tired surroundings?*

If so, you've come to the right place; here you'll find answers to these and many other questions. How to Build Paths, Steps, and Footbridges guides you through the nitty-gritty, how-to aspects of building paths, steps, and footbridges but also gives you insight to aesthetic considerations. Guiding you step-by-step from initial musings, through the design process, and finishing up with the actual construction, this book can help you create something that's not only functional but also a pleasure to behold and experience.

With a little guidance, and perhaps some professional help, anyone can complete these projects. They don't require a workshop full of fancy tools, many of the requisite skills are easy to learn, and construction tolerances often don't have to be especially precise to obtain excellent results. Paths, steps, and footbridges make excellent family projects, and perhaps best of all, when done well, they help us recapture and share a sense of joyful wonder.

ACKNOWLEDGMENTS

I thank the following friends and family: David Vreeland, my business partner and dear friend, who was always available to answer my questions and provided most of the structural information for this book; Phyllis Jeswald, my wife, who provided feedback for the early chapters and good-naturedly listened for a year and a half to talk of paths, steps, and footbridges; Jonas and Liza, my children, who have forgiven me for building the bridge *after* they left the house; and Hester Jeswald, who, with her considerable knowledge of the industry, helped me navigate the complex world of publishing.

I thank the following people for helping me with the design and construction of my path, steps, and footbridge: Mark Wolfram and Richard Bernie of Wolfram Tree and Landscape Service; Mark Ladd and Douglas Upton of Mark Ladd & Son Construction; and Nina Newington of Nina Newington Garden Design.

I thank the following people and businesses for taking time out either to read parts of the manuscript or to answer my questions: Ted Corvey, Marketing Director, Pine Hall Brick, Winston-Salem, North Carolina; Jim Hawkins, Inspector of Buildings, Franklin County Cooperative Inspection Program, Greenfield, Massachusetts; Brian Lashway, Lashway Logging, Inc., Williamsburg, Massachusetts; Daniel Ziomek, Nursery Manager, Hadley Garden Center, Hadley, Massachusetts; Jay Savage, Vice President, Savage Sod Farms, Deerfield, Massachusetts; Ginger Warren and the staff at Rugg Lumber Company, Hatfield, Massachusetts; Mickey Grybko, Sales Manager, Amherst Farmers Supply, Amherst, Massachusetts; Brian Foote and the staff at Cook Builders' Supply, Easthampton, Massachusetts; the staff at Amherst Woodworking, Northampton, Massachusetts; the staff at Cowls Lumber, Amherst, Massachusetts; and Jeff Easterling, Northeastern Lumber Manufacturers Association, Cumberland, Maine.

Imagine the Possibilities

PATHS, STEPS, AND FOOTBRIDGES — when well executed — can help transform any yard into a much-loved garden sanctuary. How? They enhance and organize outdoor spaces by providing pleasing focal points and useful links between different areas. And they immerse us in our surroundings, helping us enjoy all that our home landscapes have to offer.

The photographs in this chapter represent just a sampling of possible designs and uses. Study them to see which you like best, then ask yourself why you find them so appealing. Is it the way they make you feel when you look at them? Do you experience a sense of serenity and tranquillity, perhaps? Or is it the practical aspects — the layout, materials, plantings, or some combination of these elements — that catch your eye?

Next, consider which elements you want to incorporate in your design. At this point, the sky's the limit. Keep your mind open and imagine what your ideal project or projects might be. I provide a brief overview of paths, steps, and footbridges in this chapter, then address the formal planning process in chapter 2.

▲ Destinations make paths inviting. Here, a stepping-stone path emerges from a simple floral border and ushers the walker down a few steps to the edge of a quiet pool.

▶ Juxtaposing formal and informal elements heightens visual interest. The turned posts and balusters of this footbridge serve as effective foils for the rugged stone steps.

▶▶ Materials contribute to mood. Sturdy, rough-hewn planks make this footbridge strong and unassuming, a perfect complement for a well-traveled, bark-mulch path through a lush woodland setting.

Paths invite us to follow. Location, context, and intended use will help you decide which path type, design, and materials are most appropriate for your particular needs. For example, in a casual garden, a simple, unobtrusive stepping-stone path is a good choice. To welcome visitors to a front door, a formal, intricately patterned brick walkway with well-defined edges is fitting. A path that serves a strictly utilitarian function, such as one that leads from a garden to a tool shed, should be durable and smooth to accommodate heavy wheelbarrows and garden carts.

◄ This stepping-stone path is awash in texture and color. The purple and pink plantings appear to tumble over and around the path, while various shades of green contribute to its haphazard, patchwork feel.

► The herringbone pattern of this formal brick entryway urges the walker forward, while the narrow, curved path offers a pleasant detour around the flower bed. Using a material other than brick for the front steps would have accentuated the sense of arrival.

▼ The gentle curve of this walkway offers relief from the rigid, geometric pattern of the flagstones. Judicious plantings direct the eye and echo the curves of the path.

► Large, smooth stepping-stones provide generous, stable footing and accommodate a variety of stride lengths. A regular, predictable pattern such as this doesn't demand as much of the walker's attention as an irregular pattern would.

◄ Delicate rock garden plants, and fallen blossoms, offer a delightfully striking counterpoint to the cold, hard surface of the stepping-stones.

► Small stepping-stones with irregular surfaces make walking a challenge. Unless we pause for a moment, we tend to see only those things directly underfoot when walking such a path.

► Edges help to define a path. In this example, there are three types: to the right, a stone border between the path and the flower bed; to the left and barely visible, a low retaining wall; and in the foreground, perhaps the most striking of all, the grass. The taller plantings on either side of the path also help to define it, but notice how some branches reach into the space of the walker. This may add an air of mystery or may quickly become an annoyance.

► Another advantage of wide, regular stepping-stones is their utility. They can easily accommodate a wheelbarrow or garden cart .

◄ Relative scale is an effective design tool. A pebbled path with flagstone border is the perfect backdrop for this effusive display of petunias and ornamental grasses.

▼ Varying material size, color, and pattern of installation adds texture and interest to a path; a monolithic slab, by contrast, would dominate its surroundings. Varying path width, using large plantings, and allowing plants to encroach on the path also influence visual impact.

When selecting materials, always think about how the path will be used and what you want it to look like. Do you want the path to complement its surroundings or contrast with them? Is a finished, formal look your goal or are you hoping for a more more casual, natural-looking result? Stone, masonry, mulch, wood, even grass — used alone or together — can all be effective choices depending on your particular needs. Consider the materials your palette and the ground your canvas.

▲ Contrasting colors and textures demand attention. Here, patio blocks are set in a bed of pea stone, combining the formal with the informal.
▶ Be creative in how you use and install materials. Wood rounds, stone flagging, cobblestone, even intricate stone mosaics each can be used to great effect.

Paths are not merely routes of travel but also enticements for the senses. Incorporating features that engage and delight the eyes, ears, and nose enhances a path's appeal.

Plants and ground covers breathe life into their surroundings, adding color, texture, movement, and fragrance and encouraging visitors to linger.

▲▲ It takes time for ground covers to fill in the gaps among stepping-stones, but when they do, the result can be stunning.

▲ This bountiful floral border promises a visual and aromatic treat. The jewel tones complement the subdued colors of the formal brick walkway.

▶ Ornamental grasses add height, movement, and sound to the edges of this path. The subtle shades of green and yellow contrast wonderfully with the cool blues and grays of the gravel path.

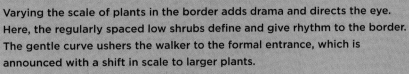

Varying the scale of plants in the border adds drama and directs the eye.
Here, the regularly spaced low shrubs define and give rhythm to the border.
The gentle curve ushers the walker to the formal entrance, which is
announced with a shift in scale to larger plants.

Use like materials to establish a sense of continuity and momentum. Here, washed pea stone is used for the path and the stair treads, making for a dramatic auditory and physical transition to the soft, quiet lawn.

Fragrance creates and evokes powerful memories. When selecting flowers and plants, choose the ones you love. Fragrant path and bedding materials, such as pine needles, cedar bark mulch, and pine chips, are also excellent options.

▲ To get maximum enjoyment from your floral border, plant varieties that bloom at different times of the year. This joyous spring assortment is a feast for the eyes.

◄ Choose path materials that you enjoy. Pine needles and bark mulch are soft underfoot and have a sharp, pungent odor when the weather is hot and dry and an earthy aroma when the air is heavy and moist.

Objets d'art or found objects strategically placed along a path naturally attract the eye and direct attention. Use them as focal points or destinations to encourage further exploration.

Seating is always welcome: a garden bench or comfortable chair will quickly become a favorite resting place.

▲▲ Give visitors a destination. Comfortable seating invites rest and relaxation — the perfect way to enjoy a garden retreat.

▲ Nestled amid lush shade plants, this granite sculpture has taken on a patina befitting its prominent place in the garden.

◄▲ Planters are a wonderful way to signal a transition. Here, they mark the end of the path and the beginning of the steps. Attract birds by choosing plants that offer cover and food, and by incorporating bird feeders and birdbaths in your garden.

◄ An argyle path? Could be. When designing your path, keep an eye open for interesting and unusual combinations.

The shape, size, and scale of this black planter contrast sharply with the path materials and the weathered chairs. Complementary colors recede in a composition and may be overlooked, whereas contrasting colors attract the eye and demand attention.

Auditory elements add a whimsical dimension to paths. Materials such as washed stone and crushed shells click and crunch beneath walkers' feet. Chimes and bells beckon with the help of a gentle breeze. And the peaceful sounds of trickling water can be introduced with a fountain or other water feature.

▲ When planning a path, make the most of your materials. Here, a profusion of wispy, upright plants enfolds and enlivens the path, with the slightest breeze causing movement and sound. This view also demonstrates the principle of conceal and reveal, adding an air of mystery. From this vantage point, we're not certain where the path will lead.

▶ Imagine walking along this path. Now imagine how the experience would change if, instead of light-colored pebbles, the path were covered with a dark bark mulch. Which would you prefer? The log edging neatly separates the path material from the mulch.

Steps link different elevations and help us navigate steep slopes. Like paths, they can be formal or informal. Safety is always a concern with steps, so they should be functional but need not be strictly utilitarian.

◄ Climbing a long, steep set of steps can be a daunting task. Offer relief by including a mid-flight landing or turn.
▼ A spray of ornamental grasses is a striking counterpoint to these rugged, timber-and-earth steps. The rocks at the right edge not only define the steps, they also hold back the slope.

◄ Like paths, steps can be constructed from a variety of materials. Take cues from the setting, then select materials that will help you achieve the desired effect.

▼ The profusion of wildflowers on either side of these rough-hewn stone steps make for an attractive entry. The neat white gate at the top serves as both goal and destination.

Many of the techniques used to animate paths work equally well for steps. Consider the destination of the steps and the experience you want walkers to have when using them. Incorporate them artfully into hillside gardens, surround them with lush plantings, and plant crevices with moss or ground cover. Punctuate long flights of steps with generous landings and seating.

▲ As you begin thinking about your project, look for ideas that you might be able to adapt to suit the scale of your garden or yard.
▶ Because stone steps aren't always perfectly consistent in height or depth, we tend to walk with eyes downcast to ensure safe passage. Plant spaces and crevices with ground covers and moss to break up long expanses of stone. To introduce a curve in the steps, simply turn a stone or two.

Footbridges are paths across real or imaginary divides. I focus on four types of garden footbridges: plank, board-walk, joisted, and simple-truss.

Plank bridges are the most basic type. They typically cross shallow water or marshland and are usually designed to allow walkers to cross single file. If your land is high and dry, a plank foot-bridge leading to a play area can be a fun addition for the young adventurers in your family.

A boardwalk is used to navigate wet or difficult terrain and accommodates foot and wheeled traffic. If a favorite route between a tool shed and vegetable garden is frequently churned into mud, a boardwalk might be a nice alternative to a finished path. Be creative with your design. Choose a board thickness and decking pattern that will help you achieve the look you want.

▲ A plank bridge is as beautiful as it is simple. Easy to construct and durable, it can give you dry passage across wet, marshy areas.

◄ The designer of this plank footbridge cleverly offset adjacent sections to frame the flower beds and to slow down walkers.

► Each successive section of this plank footbridge rests on the previous, in effect creating a set of long, low steps.

Joisted and truss bridges span drainage ditches, small streams, and even dry swales. They also can be used decoratively in flower gardens. Railings have the greatest visual impact on these bridges, so choose an attractive style that is sturdy and functional.

▶ This railing is simple and flat. It's wide enough to accommodate a glass or bottle and sturdy enough to be leaned against.
▼ Built over the stream that feeds the pond, this bridge is the perfect spot to pause and ponder.

Small, unassuming bridges can have a big impact. Here, a series of charming little bridges gives the walker uninterrupted access to the garden and steps beyond.

Planning 2

THE KEY TO ALL successful building projects is planning. Think ahead, take stock of your resources, and expect the unexpected. Planning will streamline the process and produce superior results. Thorough and detailed planning is the surest route to a project you'll be proud of. So, as you begin to think about building your paths, steps, or footbridge, do the right thing — give your project the up-front time it deserves.

The planning process is similar for all building projects. Review the following material to familiarize yourself with the process, then read the specific chapter or chapters relevant to your project. With a solid overview, you can then return to the beginning and work through the seven planning steps.

Planning in Seven Steps

1. Identify what you want.
2. Gather information and ideas.
3. Assess your skills.
4. Prepare a preliminary budget and time line.
5. Develop a design strategy.
6. Assess the site.
7. Create a site plan.

Identify What You Want

The first step is to explore the general goals for your project and the motivations behind them. What do you want to build? Why do you want to build it? What will it accomplish? How will it be used? Who will use it?

Maybe you'd like your garden to have more definition or structure. If so, a path might be the answer. Or perhaps the entry to your front door slopes up or down too steeply and would be safer with steps. And what about that gully in the backyard that makes getting to the vegetable garden so awkward? A small bridge would make the trip easier and also add charm to your property.

Ask yourself these questions to stimulate your thinking and generate ideas.

■ *What practical needs do you want to address?*
■ *Do you have aesthetic goals to achieve? Are they the main purpose of the project, or secondary?*
■ *How do you use, or want to use, your property? Are you making use of the space you have for the activities that are most important to you? Consider everyone who will use your property, especially children, the elderly, and anyone with disabilities.*
■ *Are there desirable features on your property that deserve to be highlighted? A special tree or view, for example? Conversely, are there features you want to either downplay or cover up? Many yards would benefit from more privacy or from screening out a busy street.*
■ *What is the style of your house, and what is the nature of the surrounding landscape?*
■ *What are your style preferences: informal, casual, whimsical, rustic? Or are they mimimalist, understated, restrained, and formal, or some combination?*

Gather Information and Ideas

Once your goals are firmly in mind, it's time to brainstorm. Turn your imagination loose, and don't let inexperience or budget limit ideas. Study landscaping magazines and books for ideas, and keep your options open. This will help you consider the widest range of possibilities early in the process when you can use them. Later, when you begin to design your project, you will evaluate your options more critically.

To assist with brainstorming, familiarize yourself with as much information as you can, and seek advice and input from as many people as you can. Starting at home is always a good idea. Typically one person in the household is the driving force behind a project. If that person is you, however, don't go it alone. Let your family and friends know what you want to do. They can serve as sounding boards for your ideas and will probably be a refreshing source of new ideas.

If you gather most of your information from books and the Internet, it's inevitable that some of the ideas won't be appropriate for your particular location. To infuse a local perspective into your idea gathering, study your neighborhood, notebook and camera in hand. If you see something you like, ask the homeowner about it. Inquire about what went well, what didn't go well, and costs. Most people are happy to talk about their projects.

Begin to familiarize yourself with the types of materials you might use for your project. Spend an afternoon wandering around a building, landscaping, or home-supply store. Lift some stepping-stones, notice the textures of the different masonry pavers, and check out the supply of rot-resistant woods. Inquire about availability, suitable uses, and general pricing. (See chapter 3 for a general overview of materials and tools recommended for the projects in this book.)

Last, consider your personal style. How do your tastes mesh with the style of your house and property? How will you integrate the new with the old? If you're unsure, notice details that catch your eye and ask yourself what it is about them that is most compelling. Do they have something in common? Are they consistent with your preferences, or do they help refine and define them?

All of this prospecting will broaden your palette of ideas. It will also generate enthusiasm and excitement.

KEEP ORGANIZED

Organizing the ideas you collect — the pictures, photographs, and notes — is important. With everything accessible in a filing system or loose-leaf binder, you'll be far more likely to find and make good use of the material you collect. There's nothing worse than trying to locate a picture of that "perfect" brick pattern and not being able to find it. Organized reference materials also will be invaluable during the design process.

◼ Assess Your Skills

Paths, steps, and footbridges are perfect do-it-yourself projects, but they're not always simple. As a part of the planning process, do some self-assessment. What skills do you have? Do you have a strong back? Can you handle power tools? Are you comfortable with basic math? Do you have an artist's eye? Often, the greatest success comes to those who know when to ask for help.

As a designer, builder, and "weekend" builder of stone walls and paths, I considered myself fairly qualified to undertake the construction of the paths, steps, and footbridge on my property. Still, it was spring and I was eager to complete these projects as soon as possible, so I sought experienced help. I hired a stonemason to help with the stone wall, path, and steps, with the understanding that I would work with him. A carpenter friend agreed to help me with the bridge, and I consulted a master gardener for help with plant selection and layout. For reasons of efficiency and expertise, you also might want to seek help for part or parts of your project.

A Work in Progress

A year after my son's sixth birthday, we began to build a pond adjacent to our house. We had wanted to build it before constructing the house, but some level-headed friends persuaded us that we should have a roof over our heads before we created a home for trout. After a year of construction — drawn out by stuck bulldozers, an atypical "rainy season," and a long New England winter — the pond was finished, but our work was just beginning.

That first year we imported sand for a beach, which became the new starting point for a path that led to the island across the brook. We also cleared the banks of stones and broken branches and planted a mix of field grasses and wildflowers.

The beach is about 75 feet away from our house and the grade to it is fairly steep. We wanted to make beach access easy and inviting, so we planned to use a combination of paths and steps.

We hired a stonemason to complete a large stone retaining wall that I had started a few years earlier. The adjacent paths ended above the sloping access to the beach. Here the mason built a useful set of wide stone steps.

Over the next several years, I built a series of small walls to create flower and vegetable garden terraces on either side of the steps and carved two narrow footpaths that arced around one side of the pond; one was right at the water's edge and the other tunneled through the bordering hemlocks.

It was all coming together quite nicely, but a few things were missing: a raft, a dock, and a bridge. The first two were easy. One summer, the kids and I built a raft and a dock from reclaimed old-growth cedar and recycled 30-gallon plastic drums. But the bridge was another matter. Each winter I'd tell them that we'd build the bridge that coming spring. But each fall would end bridgeless.

It wasn't until I found myself with grown children and more free time that I built the bridge. Whatever your situation, keep in mind that you can work on your project in phases as your motivation, budget, and time allow.

Prepare a Preliminary Budget and Time Line

Your budget is obviously a key factor, so it makes sense to create a preliminary one early in the process. Fortunately, proper planning can help you spend less and get more.

By now you probably have a general idea of what you're planning to build. If so, start your budgeting by assigning an amount that you would like to spend on your project. Make allowances for design, consulting, labor, and materials. Consider the pricing information you've gathered from suppliers, friends, and neighbors, and try to be as realistic as possible. If you're interviewing professionals to help you with certain aspects of the project, ask them for rough estimates. It's too early in the process to expect precise cost estimates, but you need to know that your preliminary budget is at least in the ballpark. Later, revisit your budget.

Next, assess the time you have available to work on the project and decide what an ideal time frame for the project might be. Are you hoping to have the project done in time for a Fourth of July picnic, for example, or is your time frame more open ended? Will weather or changes of season affect your work? A manageable time line can help you plan your work and gauge your progress; it can also be a powerful motivator if you need one.

Develop a Design Strategy

Whether your project is large or small and whether you plan to hire design professionals or do it all yourself, you'll find it worthwhile to approach the design process much as a professional would.

Consider the Big Picture

Begin by stepping back and taking a broad perspective. For example, do a rough layout of a path before you start designing an intricate paving pattern. Likewise, be certain a stair location fits with the overall plan before spending time calculating a precise riser dimension. Define the general "feel" of your bridge before focusing on the structural aspects.

I begin by making sketches, exploring initial ideas with loose, free-hand drawings. Tissue tracing paper works well for this exercise: it's cheap, so I can use lots of it, and I can build on my ideas by tracing them and then amending them with overlays of succeeding solutions. Tracing paper is a useful tool to help you consider various options.

Consider Multiple Options

One of the biggest challenges I encountered early in my design career was getting overly attached to the first thing I put on paper. It took several years for me to understand that an initial design is just a first draft, and that a better solution often appears in the next version. Even if I ultimately end up with something that's close to my initial effort, exploring other options usually enriches the final solution.

Try several designs on paper before committing to one. For every design or major element within a design, try to come up with at least three options. Try out paths and steps of varying widths and shapes. Curve them, angle them, taper them. Do the same for a bridge: investigate different profiles, railing patterns, and post configurations. Experiment with how different materials will impact the designs. Notice how the topography shapes your design: What challenges does it present? How can you use it to your advantage? Don't worry about making scaled drawings at this stage. A series of freehand sketches is all you're looking for right now. When you have options that you'd like to investigate further, move on to drawing to scale with the aid of your drafting equipment.

While doing all this paperwork is very important, you should also explore your options at the site itself. Use string and stakes or a garden hose to outline paths or mark the location of proposed steps. Span a proposed bridge site with a sturdy board or an extension ladder. These techniques will help you get a sense of what the finished project will feel like in three dimensions, and you'll be better able to judge the pros and cons of one design over another.

Let Go of Perfection

As you consider and evaluate the various design options, you may begin to notice that seldom do things work just the way you thought they would. What looks good on paper may not feel right in three dimensions, or perhaps it just won't fit the location the way you had hoped. Don't be discouraged. Designing is a process and usually requires a series of compromises that, after all the factors are considered, lead to the best possible solution. "Best possible" is the operative phrase here because, in my experience, a "perfect" design solution, one that fully meets all requirements, is not possible, and to search for one is fruitless. Know that perfection is not attainable — it might not even be desirable — and that if you follow through with proper planning, you'll come up with an excellent plan and finished project.

Put It on Paper

An important part of any design process is committing ideas to paper, and this means doing some drawing. Don't be intimidated by the thought of drawing. Drawings — no matter their quality — will help you refine and communicate your ideas in a way that's impossible with words.

You don't need any special drafting equipment to create the type of drawings you'll need for these projects, but the right tools will certainly help speed things along. All this equipment can be purchased at well-stocked art- or office-supply stores. Mail-order or Internet catalogs make it easy to locate what you need, but I find it helpful to buy in person so that I can get a sense of how the item feels in my hand.

■ **Architect's scale.** An architect's scale assists in drawing objects "to scale," that is, reduced in size to fit on the paper. For example, if an object that is 1 foot long is drawn ¼ inch long on paper, it's drawn to a ¼-inch scale. The familiar triangular architect's scale has ten scales of measure and a standard ruler.

■ **Drafting board.** You don't need a full-sized drafting table, but a small drafting board is a useful tool. Most of the drawings for these projects, if drawn to an appropriately sized scale, should fit on 11 × 17-inch paper, so an 18 × 24-inch drafting board should work well.

■ **T-square.** If you are going to do your drawings on unlined paper, a T-square is a handy tool to have, but it's even helpful when drawing on graph paper. Positioned on either side of the drafting board, the T-square is used to draw horizontal lines and to guide triangles.

■ **Triangles.** Triangles are used in conjunction with a T-square to draw vertical and sloping lines. Fixed triangles are available in 45-degree and 30-degree/60-degree profiles of varying sizes. An adjustable triangle is particularly useful for designing bridges. If a bridge is on your project agenda, you'll be glad to have one.

■ **Drafting compass.** This tool is used to draw arcs and circles and to transfer scaled measurements to paper.

■ **Templates.** A broad range of templates is available, some specifically for landscape drawings. Use them to draw circles and to indicate such things as curves, plants, and trees. You also might find a flexible curve helpful.

■ **Tracing paper.** Tracing paper reduces drawing time by streamlining the revision process. Simply use the tracing paper as an overlay, trace the parts of the drawing you want to keep, and make needed adjustments on the overlay. Vellum, a higher quality of tracing paper, is available from art-supply stores in sheets of varying sizes. Tissue trace comes in rolls.

■ **Graph paper.** Graph paper is lined with equally spaced vertical and horizontal lines that form a grid. The most useful size grid for our purposes is a ¼-inch grid. Graph paper is available in regular bond and tracing paper.

■ **Pencils.** Pencil, rather than pen, is the preferred drawing medium, and although it doesn't matter what type of pencil you use, the type of lead is important. Pencil leads, correctly called graphite, come in different levels of hardness. For drawings on tissue trace, HB and B work well; for vellum or bond paper, H and HB leads are a good choice. Nonphoto blue pencils are also sometimes useful, especially when doing preliminary layouts for bridge designs.

■ **Erasers.** When preparing drawings, you'll probably make some mistakes, perhaps many. White plastic erasers, available either in small rectangles or in a pen-shaped holder, do an excellent job, much better than the pink eraser found on a standard pencil.

If you don't want to buy all these tools, know that for many projects you can create serviceable drawings with a straightedge and graph paper, and that some projects can be completed with no drawings at all.

Eventually, you'll begin to feel that you've done enough legwork and research. When this happens, begin to evaluate and synthesize the information you've gathered and make some decisions about where your project is headed. This process helps you organize your thinking and define your intentions.

As you review your materials, compile a wish list for the project. It should include everything you want, even if some of it seems a bit farfetched. When you're satisfied with the list, prioritize the items by noting what you absolutely need and what you can do without. This will make decisions that will come later in the process much easier.

Assess the Site

For any outdoor project to be effective, it must work with the setting. Walk around your property and notice how the surroundings affect you. Try to get a "feel" for the environment. If possible, make these observations several times, during different times of the day, weather conditions, and seasons.

■ *Where, relative to your site, does the sun rise and set, and what path does it take along the way? How high is it in summer and how low above the horizon in winter?*
■ *From which direction do the cooling summer breezes and harsh winter winds originate?*
■ *Are there any pleasing fragrances or unpleasant odors that are present in the air seasonally or regularly? What are their sources?*
■ *Are certain areas of your property noisy and others quiet?*
■ *Are you drawn to some places on your property and repelled by others? Why? Can, or should, this be changed?*

Next, inventory the setting. Take cues from the landscape's topography — its contours and physical features, both natural and constructed, such as buildings, rocks, and trees. Keep notes on special views and unique features. You'll integrate this information in your site map or site plan.

Site-Plan Essentials

The following list details the information that should be included on a site plan. Not all items may be relevant to your plan, but more information is generally better than less.

■ **Primary existing structures, including the house, decks, porches, and outbuildings.** Begin your site plan by locating permanent structures and features because they can be used as reference points to position the others. Also note locations of windows (especially ones with important views) and all doors.

■ **Secondary existing structures, including paths, fences, walls, and garden plots.** If your project is not going to be near the house, these can also serve as reference points.

■ **Property boundary lines and construction setbacks** (the minimum distance away from property lines that structures can be built). If your project will be constructed close to your property or setback lines, you should know exactly where they are. If you have any doubts, hire a surveyor to establish the lines and check with your local building inspector about the requirements.

■ **Covenants and restrictions.** Some subdivisions regulate placement or size of structures that are within your property lines. Similarly, some cities have community-wide ordinances regarding fence or wall height, for instance.

■ **Elevation changes.** Changes in the elevation, or grade, are crucial, particularly for the design and construction of steps. Knowing the elevation of the top and toe of a slope, the pitch of a proposed path, and the difference, if any, between the two banks to be bridged is critical.

■ **Rocks and ledge.** Large rocks and ledge (solid bedrock under the ground) can cause construction challenges and opportunities, so make sure you know where they are. Use a metal rod to probe beneath the surface if you live in a ledge-prone area. (See page 89 for more on rock and ledge.)

■ **Low and wet spots.** Low spots that are subject to holding water, or "ponding," as well as areas that are frequently wet should be noted on your site plan. (See page 89 for how to address this challenge.)

■ **Trees and plantings you want to keep.** Indicate these on your plan so that you can take advantage of them and make them a part of your design. If you'll be working with contractors, you'll want to be sure to physically "flag" them with surveyor's tape so they aren't removed or damaged inadvertently.

■ **Trees and plantings you want to remove.** Again, indicate these on your plan and physically flag them (use a color different from that used for the keepers). Don't remove these items until the last minute, because you might change your mind or the design.

■ **Well, septic system, and underground pipes and wires.** It's always good to know the location of these and other buried items, but if you're going to be digging up sections of your property, it's essential. Before you dig, confirm the location of buried services by checking with utilities. See www.undergroundfocus.com/onecalldir.php or call (800) 642-2444 for a list of one-call providers by state. Once utility lines are marked in your yard with marking flags or stakes, indicate their locations on your site plan too.

Create a Site Plan

A site plan accurately outlines the borders of your property and indicates your house and other structures on it in proper scale and orientation. You may already have the beginnings of a site plan in your home ownership papers or architectural plans. If not, check with your city or town. Many keep professionally surveyed maps of neighborhoods and individual properties on file. If you can't locate any existing site or deed map, consider having it surveyed by a professional who will guarantee that the property lines are accurate.

The scope and complexity of your project will influence the tools and methods you use to measure. Site plans for simple projects of limited scope can be created using a tape measure of sufficient length and a level. But creating site plans for larger or more complex projects is easier with a transit, an instrument used by professionals to create and verify level and plumb (vertical) lines and to measure horizontal and vertical angles. (Homeowners can use a builder's level, a simpler version of the transit.)

The site plan often needs to show the horizontal location of objects as well as their vertical relationships. Highly detailed site plans use contour lines to indicate the topography, but such details aren't needed for the projects in this book. For most paths, steps, and footbridges, it's enough to know the crests and toes of slopes and whether the grade is relatively

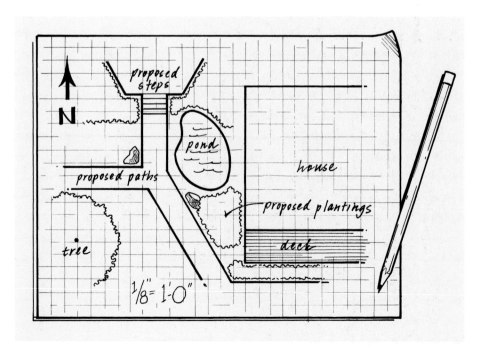

Drawn to ⅛" scale, this site plan shows an existing house, deck, pond, and shade tree. Proposed paths, steps, and plantings are also indicated. ▪

level or sloping. If you want to include contour lines on your site plan, or if your project is large and complex, you might want to consider hiring a landscape architect, surveyor, or civil engineer to do the site plan.

Lay Out the Paper

Before you begin drawing, establish the compass directions on the paper. These indicate where the sun will rise and set and the direction of the prevailing wind relative to your site. Drawing conventions usually place north at the top of the paper and south, east, and west to the bottom, right, and left, respectively.

An essential layout task is choosing the appropriate scale at which you draw your site plan. The scale depends on the size of the area that needs to be recorded and the size of the paper. Small site plans can be drawn to ¼-inch scale; ⅛-inch scale doubles the area that can be covered on the same size of paper. If necessary, small sections of a site plan can be drawn to a larger scale to show more detail.

Finally, decide where on the paper to locate the reference point or points from which the rest of the drawing will be generated. For example, if you're planning to build to the left of your house, you'd situate the house on the right edge of the paper to allow plenty of room for relevant landscape details.

To locate an object — for example, a favorite tree — in space, choose two known points (here, the northwest and northeast corners of the house) and measure to the object. Then scale the dimensions and transfer them to the site plan.

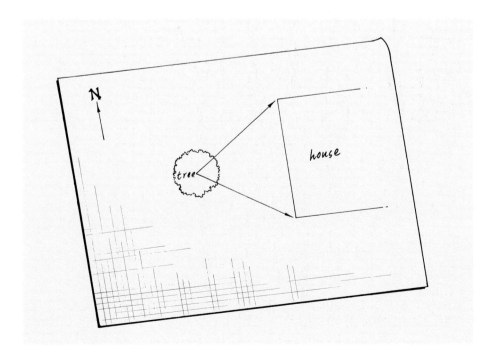

Keeping Things Square

Here are two techniques used by construction professionals to consistently guarantee accurate right angles.

The 3-4-5 method. The Pythagorean theorem ($A^2 + B^2 = C^2$) describes the relationship among the three sides of a right triangle; a right triangle has two 45-degree angles and one 90-degree angle. It turns out that right triangles with one side 3 feet long (A) and another 4 feet long (B) will have a third side (the hypotenuse) that's 5 feet long (C): 3^2 (9) + 4^2 (16) = 5^2 (25). The 3-4-5 triangle, and any other triangle with sides that are multiples of 3-4-5, will result in a perfect right angle, or square corner. This formula can be used to construct a square or rectangle and is useful if you want to build a path or locate a set of steps that will be perpendicular to your house or some other object.

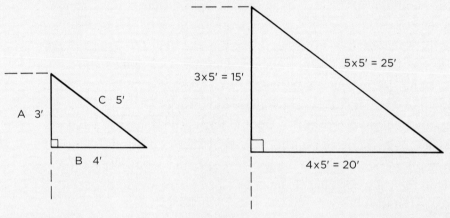

The equal diagonals method. If you're building something that's supposed to be rectangular or square, you want to make sure that it is, in fact, square and not askew. There is a simple way to do this to help ensure, for example, that your bridge frame, or even a set of on-grade steps, is square. Rectangles and squares have four equal angles and, as a result, the opposite diagonals are the same length. To square up a bridge frame, secure the frame at one end, measure the diagonals, and then shift the free end until they are equal. Note, however, that this will work only if the opposing sides are exactly the same length. So, before measuring diagonals, measure the sides. Diagonal measurements can also be used to verify the "squareness" of something that's been laid out using the 3-4-5 triangle.

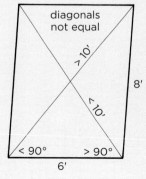
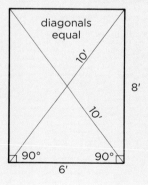

Take Measurements

Careful measurement of all physical objects on the property ensures that, when you later execute the design, specific areas will be in scale and in proper position relative to the actual conditions on the ground. To measure properly you'll need a helper — so that the tape can be held tight without sagging — and a tape that is long enough to cover the necessary distance.

Lay out the overall lot on your paper. Indicate the legal property lines as well as the public property to the curb line. Then draw your house on the property. Determine its location by measuring from the house to the side property lines. Sight down the side of the house to keep the tape straight and the measurement accurate. Transfer a point from your site — a tree or corner of a deck, for instance — to your plan by measuring to it from two known points and then transferring those measurements to paper. Then proceed to measure everything on your lot, including high and low points, wet and dry areas, winds, views, and exposure.

If you've taken time to work through the information in this chapter, congratulations! You've given pre-construction planning the time and attention your project deserves. Whether you're building a path, some steps, or a footbridge, you can rest assured that you've made the best start possible.

Tools & Materials

3

A SIGNIFICANT PIECE of the construction puzzle involves tools and materials. Just as it is important to understand the topography of your property — the "raw" elements of design — so it is important to become familiar with the wide range of available building tools and materials before you consider your project in more detail.

Tools of the Trade

Construction professionals and tradespeople understand that a task can be completed more accurately and efficiently if they use the proper tool for the job. You need not outfit yourself like a professional, but having appropriate tools, or access to them (specialized tools can often be rented), will make your projects more enjoyable and less frustrating.

Another lesson to be learned from professionals is that quality matters. That's why they like to buy the highest-quality tools they can afford, and you should, too. High-quality tools are finely crafted, well balanced, and durable, and they help to produce quality work.

You probably won't need every tool on the lists that follow, so review them in their entirety, then match the work you're planning to do with the tools you will need. If you'll only need to use a tool once or twice, or if it's expensive, consider renting it. The tools are organized by the task performed; the uses described are specific to the projects in this book.

Measuring and Layout

Measurements for paths, on-grade steps, and bridge building may not have to be as precise as those required for finish carpentry, but you'll still want your work to be reasonably level, aligned, and properly spaced. These tools can help you accomplish that.

- **FOLDING STICK RULE:** *Six or 8 feet long; used for measuring short distances or individual rocks, bricks, and boards.*
- **TAPE MEASURES:** *A 25- or 30-foot tape measure is the standard; a 100- or 200-foot tape measure is useful when longer distances need to be measured, such as during site-plan layout.*
- **LEVELS:** *A 2-foot level is used for leveling individual stones or bricks and a 4- or 6-foot for leveling longer distances, such as the entire width of a path or stairs.*
- **LINE LEVEL OR SIGHT LEVEL:** *Used for determining grade heights or ensuring level installations over long distances.*
- **BUILDER'S LEVEL AND TRANSIT:** *A builder's level is a site level mounted on a tripod and, like a site level, can be used to find grade heights. A transit, or theodolite, can measure horizontal and vertical angles and precisely locate objects in space, providing information that allows those objects to be plotted on paper.*
- **MARKING EQUIPMENT:** *Wooden stakes (3 to 4 feet long) or pin flags, string, garden hose, and marking paint can be used to indicate locations, edges, and heights.*

Earth Work

Truth be told, digging is one of my favorite activities, and high-quality tools certainly make a big difference here.

■ SHOVELS: *Round-nosed for digging holes and moving material, and square-nosed for leveling, peeling back sod and grass, and moving loose material*

■ POST-HOLE DIGGER: *For digging small-diameter holes; diggers with serrated or beveled edges work best.*

■ DIGGING BAR: *This 5- to 6-foot-long bar has a small blade at the end; useful for prying rocks and cutting small roots.*

■ FORKS: *Pitchfork or hayfork (thin tines) for lifting bark mulch, and a digging fork (wide tines) for turning over earth.*

■ RAKES: *Bowhead garden rake and aluminum landscape rake.*

■ HOE: *Long-handled for scraping and moving fill and earth.*

■ EDGER: *A long-handled model for cutting turf.*

■ MATTOCK OR PICKAX: *For breaking through really hard soils, cutting roots, or prying stones.*

■ AX OR HATCHET: *For cutting the occasional root.*

■ HAND TAMPER: *For compacting small areas of fill or soil.*

■ ROLLER: *For compacting larger areas of fill or soil.*

■ VIBRATING PLATE COMPACTOR: *For compacting gravel and sand fill and for settling pavers.*

■ KNEE PADS: *This type of work requires a lot of kneeling, and kneepads serve as shoes for the knees.*

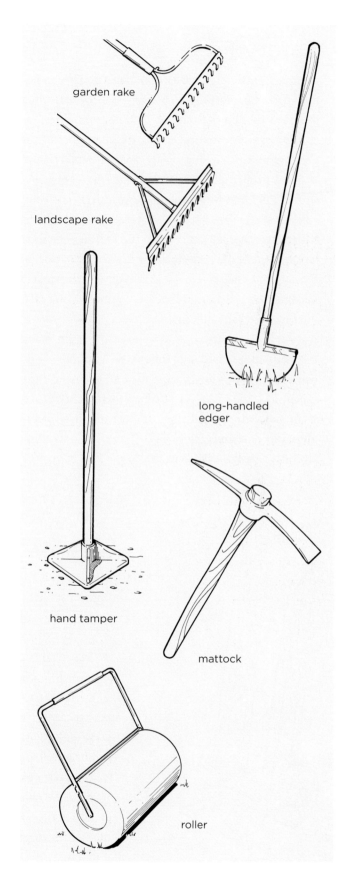

garden rake

landscape rake

long-handled edger

hand tamper

mattock

roller

Safety First

An injury puts more than a damper on a project, and one trip to the emergency room can be painful, literally and figuratively. So before you turn a shovelful of dirt, lift a rock, or strike a single hammer blow, ensure your personal safety.

■ **Protect your eyes and ears.** Wear safety glasses while cutting, splitting, or shaping stone, masonry, or wood, and also wear properly rated ear protection when using power tools.

■ **Wear proper clothing.** Wear rugged gloves to protect your hands from abrasive stone and masonry surfaces and from wood splinters. Wear pants and shirts that fit snugly to reduce the likelihood that you will snag a pant leg or catch a sleeve; tuck in shirts for the same reason. Wear sturdy work boots with a heavy lug sole for traction and to lessen the impact of a dropped tool or stone.

■ **Keep the work area clear of hazards, including building materials and tools.** To work efficiently, you need to have a selection of your chosen building materials nearby to pick from. If your materials are not properly piled or controlled, however, your work zone could become a danger zone, inviting nasty falls and sprained ankles. Unused tools lying around are also potentially dangerous. At the end of the workday, excavations of any depth should be cordoned off with rope or plastic fencing.

■ **Read, understand, and follow the manufacturer's instructions before using power tools.** Manufacturers provide instructions for a reason. Also, don't use a tool that is broken or has missing parts, especially if the broken or missing part is a safety feature such as the blade guard on a circular saw.

■ **Maintain focus and allow ample time for projects.** Construction of any kind is dangerous and physically demanding; give tasks your full attention. If time gets short, be patient and don't rush; haste is a major cause of accidents. If you get tired, stop working for the day and start fresh tomorrow.

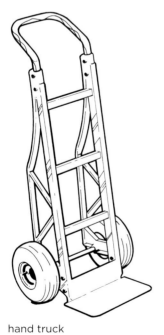

hand truck

Lifting and Moving

Constructing paths, steps, and footbridges requires a lot of heavy lifting and moving. You'll save time, energy, and perhaps your back if you invest in the appropriate tools.

■ STEEL PRY BARS: *Small crowbar and flat bar for adjusting stones and beams; 4- or 5-foot-long steel bar for prying large rocks.*

■ GARDEN CART: *For carrying large quantities of relatively light materials such as bark mulch and pine needles.*

■ WHEELBARROW: *For transporting dirt, small rocks, and gravel; I recommend a heavy-duty model with "tip-stop" bar and pneumatic tires.*

■ HAND TRUCK: *Great for moving large rocks and bags of sand, especially when equipped with pneumatic tires.*

■ BUCKETS: *For carrying sand, gravel, and other materials in small quantities; discarded joint compound buckets are ideal for this purpose, and free.*

Tools for Cutting and Shaping Stone and Masonry

If you don't own these tools, this is a perfect opportunity to get some good ones. Some of these you're probably better off renting or borrowing.

- **SLEDGEHAMMERS:** *A long-handled 8-pound sledge for breaking large rocks and a 3-pound sledge for smaller rocks and driving chisels and wedges.*
- **BRICK MASON'S HAMMER:** *For trimming the edges of stone and breaking bricks.*
- **STONEMASON'S HAMMER:** *For breaking stone or masonry or hitting a chisel.*
- **STONE CHISELS:** *A 2½-inch-wide chisel for splitting rocks and a 1½-inch chisel for cutting and for trimming edges.*
- **MASON'S SET:** *A chisel with one beveled edge, used for breaking masonry materials.*
- **RUBBER MALLET:** *For tapping stone and brick into place.*
- **CIRCULAR SAW:** *For cutting masonry when equipped with a dry-cut masonry blade.*
- **CUT-OFF SAW:** *A handheld, gas-powered saw that cuts with a circular blade.*
- **TABLE SAW:** *For cutting masonry when equipped with a dry-cut masonry blade.*
- **WET SAW:** *Stationary saw; blade is bathed with water as it cuts.*
- **GUILLOTINE CUTTER:** *For rough-cutting concrete pavers and tile.*

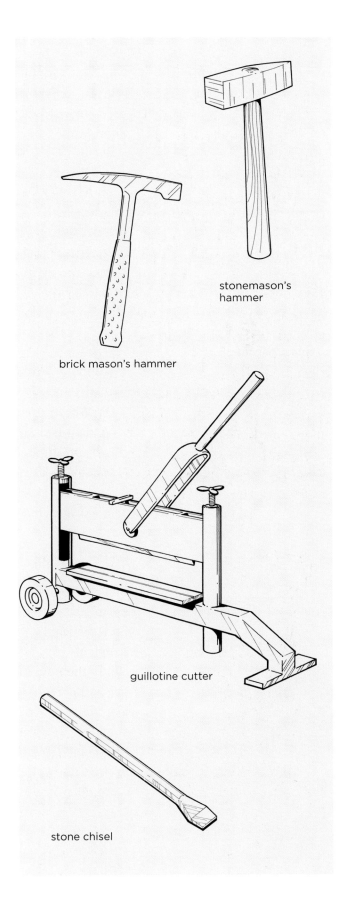

stonemason's hammer

brick mason's hammer

guillotine cutter

stone chisel

Tools for Working with Wood

Most do-it-yourselfers have at least some of the following tools. If you don't have a particular tool and always wanted one, now might be a good time to buy it. Upgrading to higher-quality tools might also be appropriate.

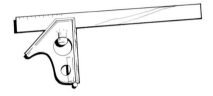

combination square

■ HAMMERS: *Sixteen-ounce finish and 20-ounce framing hammer; curved claws are good for pulling nails, while straight claws are better for prying.*

■ HANDSAWS: *An eight-point crosscut saw for rough work and an eleven- or twelve-point saw for finer work.*

■ CIRCULAR SAW: *A model requiring a 7¼-inch blade is a good choice; carbide-tipped blades are best for cutting wood, and diamond blades will cut masonry and stone; fairly powerful cordless saws are now available.*

■ STATIONARY SAWS: *A table saw is good for ripping and crosscutting; a "chop" saw is good for crosscutting.*

■ ELECTRIC DRILL: *A cordless ⅜- or ½-inch drill with an extra battery and a variety of drill and screwdriver bits is best for projects in this book.*

■ WOOD CHISELS: *For finishing notches and cutting recesses; a 2-inch and a 1-inch chisel should suffice.*

■ SQUARES: *To mark lines and calculate stairs, you may need a framing square, an adjustable 12-inch combination square, or a "speed" square.*

■ MISCELLANEOUS: *A few hand screwdrivers, a wire brush, nail sets, chalk line, and nylon string.*

Choosing Appropriate Materials

The choice of building materials plays a critical role in the relative success of a building project. Paths, steps, and footbridges can be beautifully designed and integrated into the surroundings, but if they are constructed with materials that don't fit the function, won't last, or are difficult to maintain, their beauty is only superficial and potentially fleeting. Don't undermine your hard work by using inappropriate or inferior materials. Take time to evaluate and choose them carefully.

Functional Considerations

Appropriate materials should complement function, not fight it. For example, pea stone for a path to your front door is probably not a good choice. Individual stones can get stuck in shoe treads and be tracked into the house. Other loose-fill materials, such as pine needles and bark mulch, often are tracked into houses. So, unless you want to add to your cleaning chores, it would be wise to keep such materials a distance from the house.

If you live in an area with snowy winters, take snow removal into consideration when choosing materials. Stone paths and steps are difficult to clear with a shovel.

Another aspect to keep in mind is the "underfoot" experience. Materials for front or back doors should provide firm, stable footing. If people walking on a path, steps, or footbridge are likely to be barefoot, sharp stones or rough wood prone to splintering should be avoided.

Durability

Some materials age better than others. When materials age gracefully, we say they develop "character" or achieve a nice patina. Paths, steps, and footbridges need to stand up to the environment and should be constructed with durable, rot-resistant materials, but you should also try to choose materials that age gracefully. As a general rule, materials that try to fight the elements rather than yield slowly to them don't age well. For example, mortared joints and poured concrete slabs are rigid and, no matter how carefully they are built, will invariably develop unattractive cracks.

Maintenance

While it may not be possible to build maintenance-free paths, steps, and footbridges, you can choose and install materials with the goal of minimizing the maintenance they will require. For example, you can design paths and steps so that you can easily mow up to the edges and over the surface (in the case of paths), thus reducing the time spent trimming. Raking leaves and shoveling tend to scatter loose-fill materials beyond their intended borders, requiring periodic replenishment.

Ease of repair is another maintenance-related issue that is affected by both the choice of material and the construction techniques. When a concrete slab develops cracks, for example, it is virtually impossible to do an attractive repair; but if an individual piece of flagstone or a paver breaks, it can easily be removed and replaced. Likewise, mortared joints cannot be repaired as easily or attractively as dry-fit construction.

Green building guidelines

To lessen the environmental impact of your work, use earth-friendly, or "green," building practices that minimize consumption of nonrenewable resources, maximize use of renewable resources, and do not contaminate the environment.

Products made from environmentally attractive materials

CATEGORY	MATERIALS/APPROACH	RESULT
Salvaged products	Recycled brick, timbers	Save raw materials and production energy
Materials with recycled content	Composite materials, glass	Reduce waste stream
Locally available/native materials	Stone, wood, chips, pine needles	Use less energy to transport, more awareness of manufacturing processes
Industry by-products	Oyster/clam shells, bark mulch, wood chips	Reduce waste stream
Products from sustainably managed forests	Lumber	Promotes long-term viability of forests

Products that are green because of what they don't contain

CATEGORY	MATERIALS/APPROACH	RESULT
Alternatives to high VOC (volatile organic compound) content	Latex-based stains and sealers	Reduce air pollution
Alternatives to conventionally preservative-treated wood	Avoid penta (pentachlorophenol) and creosote; CCA (chromated copper arsenic) is no longer available for consumer use. Use materials with naturally decay-resistant woods or other copper- or alkaline copper-based preservatives such as ACQ and CA-B (see page 62)	Penta and creosote are known carcinogens; CCA is no longer available for consumer use

Products/techniques that reduce/improve environmental impacts after construction

CATEGORY	MATERIALS/APPROACH	RESULT
Eco-friendly construction techniques	Avoid slab construction; provide gaps between path materials	Allows water to seep more readily into the ground and provides places for moss and other ground cover to grow
Design for minimum use of motorized maintenance equipment (string trimmers, leaf blowers, mowers)	Low-profile edgings and stepping-stones	Require less energy (fuel and human) to maintain
Use long-lasting materials	Stone, rot-resistant woods, rust-resistant fasteners	Reduce or eliminate the need to replace materials
Repair and/or restore damaged areas	Fix washouts and erosion; plant soil-retaining vegetation	Prevents loss of valuable topsoil and silting of water
Plan for reduced water use	Plant indigenous species that require less water; design landscape to retain water, not runoff	Conserves water

From Alex Wilson, "Building Materials: What Makes a Product Green?" *Environmental Building News* 9 (2000): 1.

Stone

When considering stone, choose the type most appropriate to your project. Stone is classified as sedimentary, igneous, or metamorphic and each is formed in a unique way. Understanding the characteristics of stone will help you remember why certain stones are used in particular applications.

Sedimentary rock is formed from sediment — such as sand, mud, and small pieces of rock — that accumulates to form layers. Over long periods of time and under the weight of additional sediment, the layers are compacted and hardened, eventually forming sedimentary rock. Sandstone, shale, and limestone are examples of sedimentary rock. Sedimentary rock is considered soft because it breaks apart more easily than other rocks, usually in layers.

Igneous rock, such as granite and basalt, is formed when molten and partially molten material cools and solidifies. Igneous rock is hard, crystalline, and difficult to work with hand tools. If you want to use igneous rock in a project, it will probably need to be precut and shaped, which will increase the cost compared to other types of stone.

Metamorphic rock, which can begin as sedimentary or igneous rock, undergoes a transformation, usually due to intense heat, high pressure, or mineral-rich fluids. Shale and limestone undergo relatively minor changes to become slate and marble, respectively, whereas schist is a crystalline form of shale that splits along nearly parallel planes.

The chart on page 48 is intended to be a general guide to stone types and characteristics. Consult with local suppliers to determine what types of stone are available in your area and which will be most suitable for your project.

Sources

One of the best ways to learn about sources of stone is by word of mouth. Perhaps a neighbor has recently built a similar project? You can also search online or in the Yellow Pages.

Try to visit several potential suppliers to look at the types of stone available. Given the high cost of transporting stone, it is usually most economical to buy stone that has been quarried nearby. Stone native to your area is also more likely to look "right" in your landscape.

It's also possible to find stone from outside your immediate area. Stone yards near my home in western Massachusetts buy from a wholesaler in Pennsylvania who carries stone from all over the United States. If there are any operating quarries near you, you can usually buy stone directly from them. Both yards and quarries typically supply stone that is suitable for

Stone types and characteristics

TYPE OF STONE	WEIGHT	WORKABILITY	STRENGTH	PROS/CONS
Granite	Heavy	Most difficult	High	Used for steps and ordered to size
Basalt	Heavy	Medium to difficult	Medium to high	Not often used for paths and steps; crushed for road-base material; also cut into tiles
Soft sandstone	Light	Easy	Low	Makes good path and step material; can be cut with a circular saw or hand trimmed
Hard sandstone, including blue-stone	Medium	Medium	Medium to high	Makes good step material; can be cut with a circular saw
Limestone	Heavy	Medium to difficult	Medium to high	Used for steps and ordered to size
Slate	Medium	Easy	Low	Easy to split but can get very slippery, and not a good choice for paths or steps; used for blackboards; good interior flooring material
Clay shale	Medium	Easy	Low	Generally too brittle for use as paths and steps; raw material used in the manufacture of bricks
Schist	Heavy	Easy	Medium	Easy to split and shape on-site and makes excellent path and step material
Marble	Heavy	Medium to difficult	Medium to high	Can get very slippery and not a good choice for paths; historically used for columns and walls in large buildings, for sculpture, and as countertops

building paths and steps, and knowledgeable employees can explain the appropriate uses for the products they carry.

If you're particularly industrious, you might consider gathering stones from your own land, farm fields, or abandoned chimneys or foundations. Depending on the amount of stone you need, gathering it can be a labor-intensive and time-consuming task, so be sure the material is suitable for your project. And by all means, before removing anything, get permission from the property owner, especially if you're eyeing an existing stone wall. Many stone walls are now legally protected because of their importance to our collective cultural heritage.

If you're going to need the help of a mason or another professional, ask around for recommendations, and be sure to interview before you hire. Ask the prospective contractor if he or she has done similar projects, then ask for names of satisfied customers and be sure to follow up with them.

The Name Game

Knowing the names and characteristics of various types of stone will help you shop. But because many types of stone are specific to particular regions, they are often given regional names. For example, the building stone that's used most often in my area is commonly known as Goshen stone, because the first local quarry to produce the stone commercially was in Goshen, Massachusetts, although now it's produced in several regional quarries. This stone, found throughout the Northeast, is actually mica schist. If I were to ask for Goshen stone in Connecticut, I would probably be greeted by quizzical looks.

Names such as *patio stone, flagstone,* and *fieldstone* are used by professionals and homeowners to identify types of stones, but this nomenclature can sometimes cause confusion. What is meant by *flagstone*? How large is it? How thick is it? Is it mica schist, slate, or something else?

Finish stone and uses

COMMON NAME	STONE TYPE	DESCRIPTION	USES
Irregular flagging or irregular flagstone	Schist, sandstone, slate	Flat stones, 1" to 5" thick, irregularly shaped	Excellent for paths and steps
Cut flagging or cut flagstone	Schist, sandstone, slate	Flat stones, 1" to 5" thick, usually cut into rectangular shapes	Excellent for paths and steps
Fieldstone	Various types of stone	Stones gathered from fields; shape and size vary depending on region	Fieldstones with one flat surface can be used for paths or steps
River stone	Various types of stone	Stones rounded by moving water	Can be used for paths
Cobblestone	Hard stone such as granite	Small stones of varying sizes, with rounded tops	Can be used for paths
Washed stone	Various types of stone	Stone washed to separate it from sand and soil; graded by size (½" to 1¾") and sometimes by color	Used as backfill in excavations for drainage and decoration; if applied thickly in paths, it can be difficult to walk on
Pea stone	Various types of stone	Washed stone, about ⅜" in diameter, sometimes sorted for color	Can be used for paths, although stones can get stuck in the treads of shoes and tracked indoors

Clear communication plays an important role in the success of a project, so be certain everyone is on the same page. To that end, when speaking with suppliers, describe the stone you want to use rather than simply referring to it by name. The "Finish stone and uses" chart on the previous page should help.

Another reason not to make assumptions about stone without seeing it is its tremendous variability in color, texture, and hardness. Differences are often pronounced in stones from the same region or even the same quarry. For example, the mica schist from quarries in Goshen is softer than that from Cummington, and the mica schist from Ashfield has a pronounced, wavy grain not found in the other two. These towns are located within a 15-mile radius of each other in western Massachu-

Utility stone and uses

NAME	DESCRIPTION	USES
Gravel (generic)	Any sandy material that contains a mix of sand and small stones	Good draining, backfill, and base material
Bank run gravel	Gravel straight from the gravel pit	May not be suitable for use in paths if it contains large stones
Screened gravel	Gravel that's screened to remove stones of designated sizes	Good base material for paths, steps, and footbridges
Processed gravel	Gravel in which the stones have been crushed to a uniform consistency	Excellent as a base for paths, steps, and footbridges; compacts well
Traprock	Dark-colored igneous rocks, such as diabase (dolerite) and basalt, that have been crushed to a specified size	Good base for paths, steps, and footbridges
Traprock gravel	Traprock that has been screened to include stone sizes from ¾ inch down to stone dust	Excellent base material that packs extremely well for paths, steps, and footbridges
Crusher run stone or rock	Sold directly as it comes from the crusher without further processing or screening	Excellent base for paths, steps, and footbridges
Crushed stone or rock	Screened and sold according to size	Excellent base for paths, steps, and footbridges
Sand, generic	Loose, granular material composed of small particles of rock	Can be used as a backfill and a base for paths, steps, and footbridges
Road sand	Coarse sand that may have been screened to remove pebbles	Infrequently used for paths, steps, and footbridges
Concrete sand	Fine-screened, washed sand	Used in concrete for slabs, pads, and footings
Mason's or masonry sand	Very fine-screened, washed sand	Used for mortar, setting beds, and dry joint filler

setts, but the stone they produce is different. If you don't like unpleasant surprises, inspect the stone for subtle, and sometimes not-so-subtle, variations before you buy it.

The stone discussed above is what I call "finish" stone, or the type of stone used to pave or that is prominent in the finished project. But you might also need to use "utility" stone — typically crushed stone, sand, or some form of gravel — for a path or foundation base. The popular names given to utility stone can also cause confusion. The definitions and descriptions in the "Utility stone and uses chart" are those typically used in the construction industry and should keep the lines of communication clear.

Working with Stone

Working with stone can be difficult, demanding, and time-consuming, so it is not for everyone. Before you take on this task, do some honest self-assessment. You might find that it makes more sense to hire a professional. In either case, it's helpful to understand how to work with stone.

There are five basic stoneworking techniques: breaking, nibbling, truing and squaring, splitting, and cutting. The technique and the tools you choose may vary according to the type of stone you're working with, but all require eye and hand protection and careful attention when working. You also will need to experiment with and fine-tune these techniques to suit the stone you're using. When working with stone, slow and steady wins the race. To avoid unnecessary lifting, work on the ground.

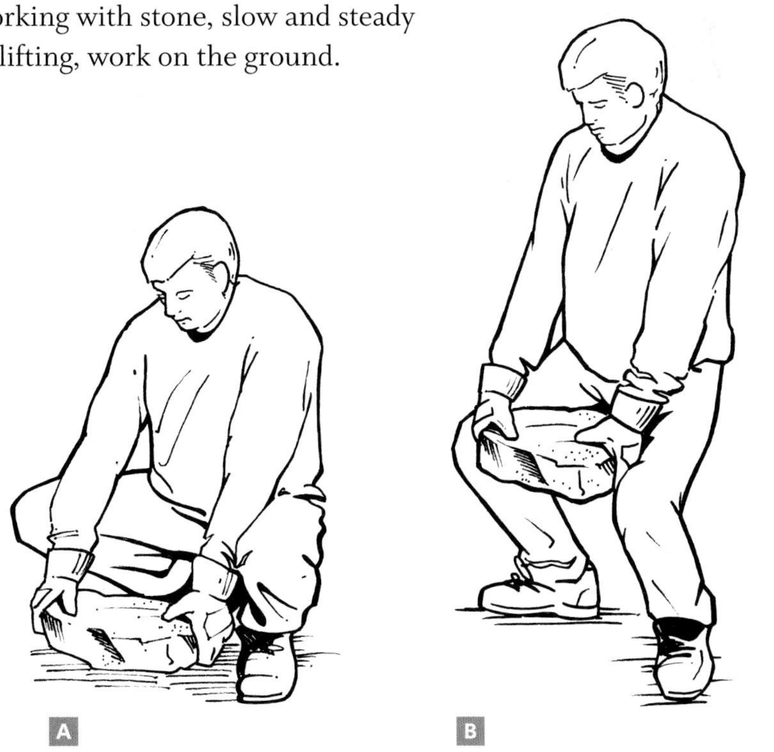

Lift with your legs, not with your back. *A.* Position yourself as close as possible to the stone and bend your knees. *B.* Grasp the stone firmly, keep your back straight, and stand, lifting with your legs.

A

B

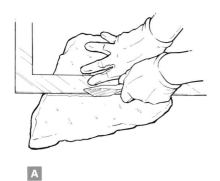

A

B

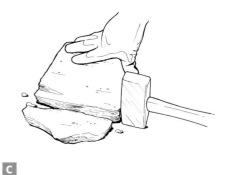

C

▲ Work patiently when breaking stone. Score it *(A)*, strike it along the line *(B)* with successively harder blows until it nears the breaking point, then use less force to finish the job *(C)*. ▧

BREAKING This technique yields the roughest result but is necessary when dividing a large stone into smaller, more usable pieces. Stone can also be broken to create shims or fill. Depending on the size of rock to be broken, you can use a stone hammer or a large sledgehammer.

First, score the stone where you want to break it. Then support it on the ground so that there is no hollow space underneath. Using the angled side of the stone hammer, repeatedly strike the stone along the line, using successively harder blows. When the stone nears the breaking point, strike it with less force. For a more precise break, strike a wide stone chisel with the flat side of the stone hammer. In contrast, an 8-pound sledgehammer will produce extremely unpredictable results.

NIBBLING When you want better control of the result, nibbling is the technique of choice. As the name suggests, nibbling involves taking small bites out of the edges of a stone, much as a child might eat a peanut butter sandwich, until the desired shape or size is achieved. It is particularly effective with the flat stones of any type, and is commonly used to construct paths and steps.

Nibbling requires a certain amount of skill, but you can develop it quickly by trial and error. Practice the technique on scrap stones, striking

▼ To develop your nibbling skills, experiment with different hammer angles: hammer flush to the surface *(A)*, hammer angled to one side *(B)*, and hammer tipped forward *(C)*. Each produces a slightly different result. ▧

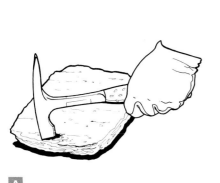

A

B

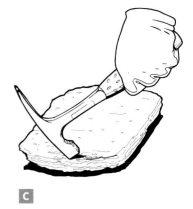

C

them with different hammer angles. With the stone secure on the ground, see how much material you can accurately remove with a single blow, without breaking too much stone.

When starting out, score a line on the stone to guide your work; with more experience, you'll be able to eyeball the desired shape. Gently strike the edge with a lightweight mason's hammer (or a small sledge-hammer if the rock is tough) to remove a bit of stone. Work your way along the edge of the stone in this manner until it's the shape you want. Try the stone in place for fit before moving on to the next stone; make any needed adjustments.

TRUING AND SQUARING *Truing*, or trimming, is a technique used to achieve a clean edge or flat surface. The best stones for paths and steps have flat, even surfaces. Occasionally, you'll find a stone that is perfect except for a ragged corner or surface bump. Truing allows you to correct this.

To true a stone, work on the ground to help absorb shock and direct the force. On the stone, score a line to follow. Use a stone hammer or a small sledge and a stone chisel. Strike the chisel lightly to establish the trim line, then work along the line using successively harder blows until the stone breaks.

If you want to true a layered stone, work from the middle of the stone rather than the edge. (Working in from the edge risks splitting off a piece that's thicker than you want, which can result in a divot or unwanted beveled edge.) Hold the chisel at a 30-degree angle and strike it gently with the hammer. Move the chisel to a new location and repeat, using slightly more force with each successive blow until the bump pops off.

Squaring, or creating angles close or equal to 90 degrees, combines nibbling and truing techniques. With a square or other straightedge, score the stone to the desired shape, then trim the stone as described above.

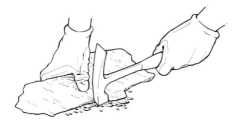

▲ Score the stone *(A)*, then gently strike the edge *(B)*. Continue nibbling until the shape is right. ▪

▲ Strike a stone chisel with a small sledge *(A)* to true a stone and achieve the desired clean edge *(B)*. ▪

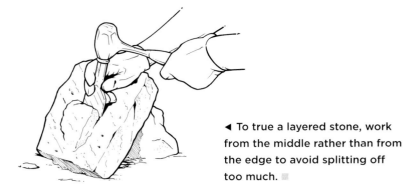

◀ To true a layered stone, work from the middle rather than from the edge to avoid splitting off too much. ▪

Sandstone has a visible grain. To split it, stand it on its edge, then gently tap a chisel along the grain with a small sledge *(A)*. As the stone splits, continue working down the stone *(B)*. ▨

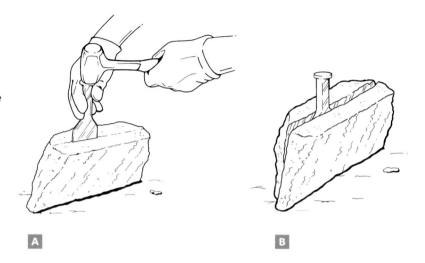

A

B

SPLITTING Rocks such as sandstone and limestone have a grain, and schist and slate form in layers. If a stone is too thick for your purposes, you can take advantage of its natural characteristics and split it.

The most precise splitting is done using a wide chisel and small sledgehammer or stone hammer. First, determine how thick a piece of stone you need. Then, pick a stone that looks appropriate and inspect the grain or layering. Stones with uniform graining, such as sandstone and limestone, can usually be split to any reasonable thickness. Results with layered stone are often less predictable.

Stand up the stone on its end and support sides if necessary to keep it stable. Working slowly and steadily, use the hammer to gently tap the chisel along the line of the grain or layer where you want the stone to split. Use just enough force to open a small fissure, then continue working down the stone as the crack widens. If you're lucky, the stone will cleave cleanly.

Occasionally, you might need only a rough split. To accomplish this, use the angled end of the stone hammer or sharp end of the mason's hammer and work down the stone the way you would with a chisel.

CUTTING Quarries and stone suppliers use powerful stationary saws to produce cut stone, but you can do the job on-site using a circular saw equipped with a diamond blade. Typically, on-site cutting is limited to flat stones. You might, for example, want to create a rectangular stair tread out of a piece of irregular flagstone.

To begin, pick a stone that is as close as possible to the shape you want and place it on two 4×4s. Then, using a framing square as a guide, mark out the rectangle you want, making sure the corners are square.

Next, set the depth of the saw blade. If the stone is an inch or less thick, you can probably cut all the way through; otherwise, plan to cut the stone halfway through, then snap it off with a gentle hammer blow. Make a test cut on a piece of scrap stone to see how well the blade cuts and if you can make the cut with a single pass.

Clamp a straightedge to the stone to guide the saw blade during the cut; a piece of plywood with its original edge will do. If you feel confident handling a circular saw or if the stone is small, you can make the cut without a straightedge. Make the first cut, set up and make the second cut in the same way, and continue working around the stone in this fashion until all cuts have been made.

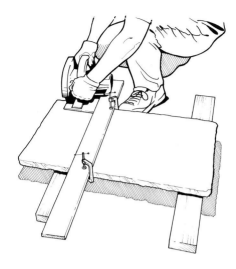

Dry-cutting a piece of stone with a circular saw creates a lot of stone dust. When cutting stone, always wear safety glasses and wear a dust mask when needed.

Masonry

When it comes to paths, the most basic masonry product is the ubiquitous paver. Although sometimes referred to as *paving brick*, the term is misleading because pavers are made from concrete as well as from brick. The standard 4-inch by 8-inch paver is surprisingly versatile and suitable for use in formal paths with regimented patterns and tight joints, as well in less formal paths with haphazard patterns, fanciful designs, or insets of tile or stone. Multiple paver patterns can be used to emphasize significant features such as an entrance or transition; see illustrations on page 56.

Pavers have a number of advantages for do-it-yourselfers. First, their relatively small size and regular shape make them easy to handle and install. As a manufactured product with fairly uniform characteristics, pavers are more predictable to work with than stone. If they are installed without mortar (dry laid), you can make changes and repairs easily. Matching colors from batch to batch is sometimes difficult, so it is a good idea to order more material than you need for a job and store the extras for future use.

Some paving patterns, such as the running bond and herringbone, direct the eye and emphasize forward motion. Others, such as the basket weave, are more static in nature. Choose a pattern that will help you achieve the effect you want. ▪

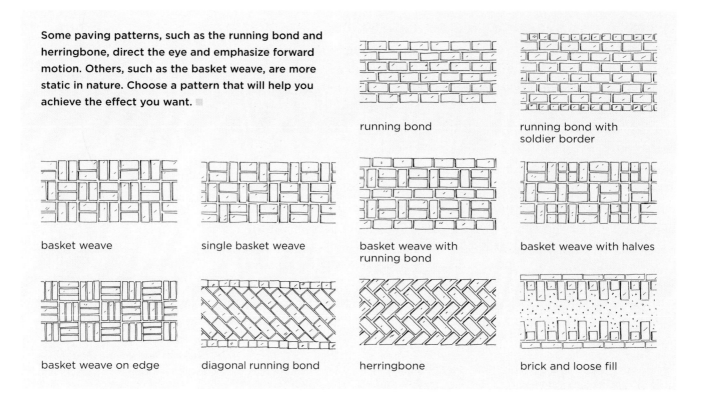

running bond

running bond with soldier border

basket weave

single basket weave

basket weave with running bond

basket weave with halves

basket weave on edge

diagonal running bond

herringbone

brick and loose fill

Brick

Brick is one of the oldest and most widely used building materials. Brick is made by firing clay to about 2000°F, which fuses the clay particles together in a permanent bond, the color of which is integral to the material and does not change or fade over time. Different types of clay, additives, coatings, firing atmosphere, and forming methods allow manufacturers to produce bricks in a broad range of colors and textures. Bricks are categorized by their intended use.

FACING BRICK Facing brick is manufactured with holes to facilitate the mortar bond. It is intended for use on interior and exterior walls. Because of the way it's formulated and fired — and the holes — it's not an appropriate option for use in paths. Recycled, solid facing bricks salvaged from older buildings might be appropriate for paths; however, they were not intended for such use and may not stand up to the task.

PAVING BRICK Paving brick is intended for use in paths and patios. Formed by either an extrusion or molding process, paving brick has high compressive strength, or resistance to crushing, and is formulated to resist water absorption and the effects of salt, chemicals, and freeze/thaw cycles. Historically, clay pavers shrank about 10 percent during the firing process, which caused troublesome size inconsistencies among batches. But today manufacturers are addressing this concern, and many now produce clay pavers with minimal size variations.

Although they are available in other shapes, most brick pavers are rectangles. There are two types: *Bonded brick pavers* are a full 4 inches by 8 inches and are meant for mortarless installation. *Modular brick pavers* measure 3⅝ inches by 7⅝ inches and are used for mortared installation. Each is sized to create a "bond," with the length equaling twice the width, when installed. Proper bonding keeps pattern lines running straight and true. Both are available in a thickness of either 2¼ inches or 1⅜ inches. Modular brick is installed with a ⅜-inch mortar joint.

Bonded bricks, when installed side by side with sand-filled joints, create a flexible, interlocking system. Some new pavers, designed specifically for sand installation, are made with spacer nibs, which simplify installation. If you want to lay brick with a wider joint than would be created by the spacer nibs, use regular bonded brick. Other types of brick are manufactured with weathered edges to simulate an aged appearance; still others have beveled edges to eliminate the chipping often associated with square-edge pavers.

Concrete

Concrete — a mixture of cement, aggregate (typically washed stone), various additives, and water — is an amazingly pliant material. Either poured on-site or precast in a factory, concrete can be formed, molded, etched, stamped, embedded, brushed, and colored to achieve an almost infinite number of effects.

POURED ON-SITE A poured concrete sidewalk or path might look fairly simple and straightforward, but extensive site preparation is required for a top-quality, long-lasting job. Because of this and the speed with which it must be installed, large jobs are best left to professionals. Additionally, monolithic stretches of poured concrete don't age well, almost always develop cracks, often break up due to the effects of freeze/thaw cycles, and are difficult to repair.

If you want to use poured concrete, start by making individual pieces of concrete flagging. Simply pour concrete into forms, let it cure, then install the separate pieces. This approach can be particularly effective when using distinctive shapes, surface designs, imprints, or embedded shells, pebbles, or tiles. Premade decorative molds are available in home centers and online.

To make your own forms, first determine the shape, size, and thickness (typically 2 to 3 inches, depending on the size) of the flagging you want. The number of forms you build depends on the size of the job and the number of pours you want to do. Next, build the forms from ¾-inch plywood. Glue and screw the two fixed sides and connect the other two sides with hinges (see illustration). During the pour, use a hook and screw eye to keep the hinged sides closed. You can also make forms from the round cardboard tubes used to form concrete piers; just cut them to the proper thickness.

You can order concrete premixed from a plant, but the amount of concrete you need at any one time will probably be significantly less than the required minimum delivery. The most efficient way to purchase concrete for small projects is to buy the dry ingredients and mix them yourself at the job site. Buy a good-quality dry mix and prepare it yourself, following the manufacturer's instructions. Concrete work can be tricky.

While it is possible to color concrete, it is in my experience extremely difficult to maintain a close color match among batches. This might not be a problem, however, if you like the effect or if the flagging will be installed with fairly wide gaps in between.

PRECAST CONCRETE Initially used to rebuild the streets of Holland after World War II, concrete pavers were not made in the United States

Use a high-quality plywood, free of knotholes and voids, to construct a form *(A)*. Fill it completely with concrete *(B)*, then let the concrete set until hard. Unhinge one side of the form for easy removal. ▥

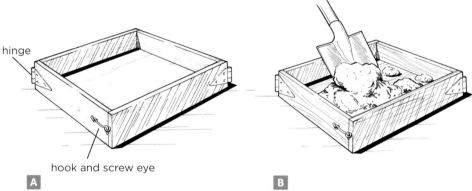

hinge

hook and screw eye

A

B

until the early 1970s. Since the late 1980s, precast concrete pavers have seen a significant rise in popularity in this country. Manufactured under high pressure and with carefully controlled ingredients, precast concrete pavers are formulated to resist breakage, freeze/thaw cycles, and even deicing salts.

Pavers are available in styles and colors (though they may fade over time) that mimic cobblestone, brick, and tile. Some manufacturers offer exposed-aggregate pavers and pavers large enough to be used as stepping-stones. Also available are concrete blocks for walls and stair treads. Concrete pavers are made with spacing nibs to facilitate installation.

Sources

Masonry materials can be purchased at lumberyards, garden-supply stores, home centers, and masonry-supply yards. It's probably best to shop at supply houses that do a large masonry business and have a knowledgeable staff receptive to do-it-yourselfers. Asking building professionals where they buy is always a good idea.

Unless a supply house is particularly large, it will probably stock only a small fraction of what's available. Browse online and if you find something that you like that's not stocked at a local yard, see if the people there can order it for you.

Working with Masonry

Many of the tools used to work stone are also used with brick and concrete pavers. The techniques are also similar, but breaking and cutting will be used most frequently. Practice the techniques on scrap pieces before starting in on your project. When breaking or cutting pavers, be sure to wear gloves and safety glasses.

BREAKING Masonry pavers and bricks do not break accurately or cleanly, so this method should be used only to make filler pieces or if you're building a rustic path. Always experiment on scrap with a method before committing to it.

For a rough break, simply lay the paver on the ground, or on sand or a carpet scrap, and strike it sharply with a mason's hammer.

Make a more precise break by using a wide mason's set (brick chisel) and hammer. Place the paver on the ground and mark the cut on all four sides. Then gently score the lines. Place the chisel on the paver face and

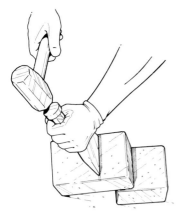

▲ Score the paver on all four sides *(A),* set it on the ground, then break it with a sharp blow. Some manufacturers recommend propping up the paver before breaking it *(B).* ▪

make the break with a sharp blow; the rough edge will be at the bottom of the paver. Some manufacturers of concrete pavers recommend supporting pavers above the ground on a surface such as wood, then striking them with a hammer and chisel to break them.

CUTTING If you are going to modify a large number of pavers or you want cleaner edges than are possible with breaking, consider cutting them. This approach is more accurate, the results more predictable, and you should be able to create smaller usable pieces. Masonry pavers can be cut with a guillotine cutter or a power saw equipped with a diamond blade. A diamond blade is more expensive than a masonry blade but does a better job.

A guillotine cutter cuts pavers faster than a saw, with one swift motion. Cutters are also quieter than power saws and do not produce the dust or paste associated with dry or wet sawing. One of the secrets of a good cut is creating a slight undercut in which the top of the paver is about $\frac{1}{16}$ inch longer than the bottom. This prevents any inconsistencies in the cut from affecting the joint. To create an undercut, mark a line on top of the paver, align it with the blade of the guillotine, tilt the paver at a slight angle, and make the cut. The edge will not be as smooth as one produced by a saw, but in many situations this is not an issue.

Smooth, accurate cuts can be made with power saws, either circular and "cut-off"-type saws, or table and stationary wet saws. Use a circular saw to cut pavers in place. Mark the pavers you want to cut with a long straightedge or chalk line, adjust the saw base to create a slight undercut (for a better fit), and make all cuts in a single pass. This approach kicks up a lot of dust, so you'll want to wear a dust mask, safety glasses, and hearing protection. As a courtesy, you might also want to tell your neighbors what you'll be doing before you start so windows can be closed if necessary.

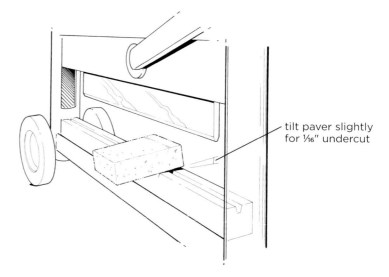

tilt paver slightly for $\frac{1}{16}$" undercut

▶ Use a guillotine cutter to cut pavers with one swift motion. ▪

Cutting that can't be executed in place is best done using a masonry table saw. This stable tool, which is available in wet- and dry-cut versions, produces the most precise cut of all. The undercut is achieved by adjusting the saw blade. The dust from dry cutting and the paste that results from wet cutting can stain concrete pavers, so if necessary, brush or rinse immediately.

▉ Wood

North America has been blessed with a relative abundance of trees, and, not surprisingly, building with wood is a part of our heritage. If forests are properly and sustainably managed, this precious resource can continue to supply us with a wide variety of building materials.

Compared to stone and masonry, wood is relatively easy to work with. That advantage comes with a built-in trade-off, however, because when used in outdoor applications, wood is not as durable as stone and masonry. Using rot-resistant varieties or chemically treated wood only delays the inevitable. For this reason, I think it's wise to use wood only if other materials cannot do the job adequately or if the costs of the other materials are prohibitive.

Fibrous Materials

Paths that feature loose-fill materials such as pine needles and bark mulch are most appropriate for informal or natural-looking garden and woodland paths. They are soft to walk on, and when wet add a woodsy smell to the walking experience. There are several loose-fill materials from which to choose.

PINE NEEDLES AND LEAVES What could be easier than having your path-building material delivered straight to the job site by Mother Nature? Well, that may be oversimplifying it a bit, but if you have conifers or deciduous trees on your property, you can use their needles or leaves to create casual-looking paths. Years ago we lived in a rented house surrounded by white pine trees, and every fall some friends would come by with their pickup truck and cart off loads of pine needles to spread on their garden paths.

A creative solution to the yearly fall task of leaf raking might be to use those leaves to create and maintain a path. Depending on the type of leaves, they can either be raked onto the path area or, if necessary, first run through a shredder. On our property, there is an abandoned town road that mulches naturally each fall, as layers of red oak and sugar maple leaves drop to the ground.

BARK MULCH Although often confused with wood chips, bark mulch is made from tree bark that has been ground up to a uniform consistency with a tub grinder or hammer mill. Sawmills remove the bark before sawing a log. Increased use of bark mulch has taken what was once a waste material that was difficult and costly to dispose of and turned it into a viable and valuable commodity. When buying bark mulch, ask about which types would be best for your purposes.

WOOD CHIPS Wood chips are made from low-quality or waste wood that has been put through a knife cutter or chipper. Standard wood chips, sometimes referred to as quarters, are about the size of a quarter and generally made from the slab wood produced when a log is squared up before it's sawn into lumber. It's my experience that this type of wood chip does not stay in place as well as bark mulch, so make sure you test it out before using it for your paths.

Chips can be made from any type of tree, and you'll want to ask what type of chips you're getting. Avoid using pine chips on paths, because they often contain a sticky sap that will become a nuisance.

A coarser type of wood chip is the *whole-tree chip*. These chips are made from treetops that are left over from logging operations or from whole trees that are too small or inappropriate to use for lumber or firewood. Whole-tree chips are not uniform in size and contain small branches and twigs. While the irregularity of chip size allows them to knit together and stay in place, they also might make for a less-than-inviting path, especially for barefoot walkers.

Another interesting result of the increased demand for wood chips has been the recycling and chipping of wood shipping pallets. Pallet chips are often colored to create a uniform product.

Solid Wood

Since the first "engineered" wood product, plywood, was introduced in the early twentieth century, modern manufacturing techniques have transformed trees into any number of incarnations, including particleboard, fiber board, oriented strand board (OSB), laminated beams, and laminated veneer lumber (LVL). Most of those products are intended for interior uses, however, and the type of wood generally used for exterior applications is just plain old solid wood right from the tree. Solid wood comes in several forms: poles, logs, and rounds; timbers and dimension stock; and boards.

Rot-resistant woods*

SPECIES	DESCRIPTION	DURABILITY
Ipé (sold under a number of brand names)	Extremely dense, tight grain, few knots; deep brown color that weathers to gray if left untreated	The highest-rated wood for insect and decay resistance
Philippine and African mahogany (includes a number of different tropical hardwoods and brand names)	Medium weight, grain pattern similar to true mahogany	More durable than cedar, but only the dark species are rot resistant
Cedar (Western red or Eastern white)	Lightweight softwood that weathers to gray if untreated	Good rot resistance

*There are a limited number of rot-resistant woods from which to choose. To increase their life expectancy, they should be treated regularly with a preservative and sealer. Always use woods that are certified as being supplied from sustainably managed forests. Redwood is a beautiful, easy-to-work, rot-resistant wood, but unless it's gathered from sustainably managed forests, it is difficult to justify its use and so is not recommended here, particularly because there are a number of suitable alternatives.

POLES, LOGS, AND ROUNDS Poles, logs, and rounds, as their names might suggest, are the least-processed wood products. *Poles*, for our purposes, can be considered tree trunks that have small diameters relative to their length. For example, a tree 4 to 6 inches in diameter and 6 to 8 feet long would be considered a pole. They can be used like landscaping timbers to create on-grade steps and low retaining walls. They can also be used decoratively to create a corduroy-type path. Poles are usually made from young trees and typically have a high percentage of sapwood, which is less durable than heartwood. Slow-growing, rot-resistant American hop hornbeam *(Ostrya virginiana)* is a good choice.

Tree trunks that have large diameters when compared to their length are called *logs*. Logs larger than 8 inches are not often used for the type of work featured in this book, but smaller-diameter logs can be used for retaining walls or in the construction of footbridges.

Rounds are slices of large-diameter logs and can be used as "stepping-stones" (see page 105). Because wood is relatively light when compared to stone or masonry, wood rounds need to be large and thick to ensure stability. Depending on the type of installation, wood rounds should be a minimum of 12 inches in diameter and 3 to 4 inches thick. Due to a tree's internal structure — trees are like bundles of straws stuck together — even if you use a rot-resistant type of wood, rounds will tend to decompose fairly quickly when they are in contact with the earth.

TIMBERS AND DIMENSION STOCK Lumber is cut and graded into four categories — beams, posts and timbers, dimension stock, and boards — according to its size, structural properties, and visual characteristics. The listed sizes are the *nominal,* or designated, sizes, not actual sizes.

If you buy lumber directly from a sawmill, it will be *rough cut.* Rough-cut dimensions can vary from one end of a piece to another by ⅛ inch to ⅜ inch or more. These variations may not be an issue with many outdoor projects, but if you want a smoother, more uniform piece of lumber, buy wood that has been *planed.* The planing process reduces the nominal size by about ½ inch, so a planed 4×4 is actually 3½ inches by 3½ inches.

Beams are intended for heavy structural use and typically support joists, walls, and rafters. Beams are at least 5 inches thick and more than 2 inches wider than they are thick. Some beams are graded for appearance as well as for strength and can be left exposed, whereas others are intended to be covered.

Posts and timbers are used for heavy structural applications. *Posts* are installed vertically and typically support beams. *Timbers* are installed horizontally, usually at the perimeter floor level. They are also used in retaining walls and on-grade steps. Strictly speaking, timbers and posts are at least 5×5 inches square and no more than 2 inches wider than they are thick. In residential constructions, however, 3×3s and 4×4s are also referred to as *posts.*

Dimension lumber is used for light construction applications, such as joists, rafters, studs, and structural planks. Many of the bridges covered in chapter 6 use at least some dimension stock. Dimension lumber is between 2 and 4 inches thick and at least 2 inches wide.

BOARDS Boards are used for trim and finish work. They are graded primarily by visual characteristics and size, and are 1 to 3 inches thick and at least 3 inches wide. Boards can be purchased in either rough or planed forms, but planed boards are best suited for our purposes.

Decking boards are a specific type of board used for exterior decks and porches. They are graded by visual characteristics, size, and strength and are 1 to 2 inches thick and at least 4 inches wide. Decking boards are strength-rated according to their ability to span a given center-to-center distance between floor joists.

Boards can be used to create boardwalks and as a footbridge decking material. Boards ripped to create small squares or rectangles are used for balusters and handrails.

Composite Lumber

In response to burgeoning interest in low-maintenance products and concerns about the safety of some pressure-treated products, the use and availability of composite decking materials have increased dramatically. Composites are made by combining wood fibers with a polymer binder. The type of polymer varies with the manufacturer and may be derived from new or recycled material; some manufacturers use recycled polyethylene. The proportion of wood fiber to polymer also depends on the manufacturer.

Composite materials have several advantages over solid wood products: they don't need stain or preservatives, they won't check or split, and they are rot resistant. Composite materials that exclusively use recycled polymers are considered "green." On the downside, they get hotter than solid wood, which might be a problem in hot and sunny areas. Also, composites are not as strong as solid wood and, in my opinion, rarely look as good as regular wood.

For the most part, composites cut and work much like solid wood, although close adherence to the manufacturer's recommendations is a must. For instance, all require screws in predrilled holes, and some use proprietary fastening systems. Typically, composites are available only as decking boards, but some companies offer composite railing systems, nonstructural posts, and even landscape timbers.

Sources

Old-growth wood that's been salvaged from deconstructed buildings is typically more durable than newly harvested wood. This can be an excellent option, particularly if you're interested in maintaining green building practices. Check for local suppliers that handle this type of wood, and check the Internet and construction magazines for sources. I used reclaimed wood to build my deck, dock, and raft.

If you own a woodlot, you might have some rot-resistant species on your property that could be cut into poles or rounds on-site or trucked to a local sawmill to be sawn into timbers or boards.

More conventional options include local sawmills that produce lumber and sell bark mulch and wood chips; garden- and landscape-supply outlets that sell wood chips, hay and straw, bark mulch, pine needles, and some solid wood materials; and lumberyards. In addition to a wide array of stocked items, lumberyards can search out and special-order items they don't normally carry. They're also likely to sell the fasteners, tools, and other equipment and materials that you'll need to do the job.

Fencing companies are another potential source of solid wood. If they build their fences with rot-resistant wood species, you might be able to buy what you need from them.

Working with Wood

While carpentry instruction is beyond the scope of this book, I'll review the fundamentals so that you can gauge your current skill level and determine whether you're ready to tackle a particular job yourself, can rapidly acquire sufficient skills, or need to hire someone to help out. The basic techniques are outlined here, with more specific details provided where appropriate in other chapters.

HAMMERING It's probably safe to say that nearly everyone has used a hammer at one point or another in his or her life. So what is there to know? Plenty. A few simple adjustments can turn potential drudgery to sheer joy.

First, choose the right-weight hammer for the job. A 20-ounce framing hammer is overkill when used to drive a small nail, while a 16-ounce finish hammer is no match for a large spike.

The right grip is also important. To achieve maximum power and leverage, don't choke up on the hammer handle; it's a waste of energy. And even though it's tempting to place your thumb along the hammer shaft for more control when swinging, try to avoid this because your thumb and hand will tire more rapidly than they would with a full grip.

Swinging a hammer, when done properly, is a graceful movement. Most of the work should be done by the forearm, using the elbow as a pivot point, with an assist by the wrist. For driving large nails, use a full arm swing with a quick snap of the wrist as the hammer strikes the nail.

To drive a nail, firmly grip the handle of the hammer, keep your eye on the nail, and swing with the forearm and wrist. ▨

Hammer smaller nails using shorter swings and a little more wrist, while wrist-only swings are used for small finish nails or hard-to-reach places. Your arm will guide the hammer where your eyes tell it to, so keep your eyes on the nail.

CROSSCUTTING Cuts that are made perpendicular to the length of a piece of solid wood — across the grain, in other words — are known as *crosscuts*. Crosscutting can be done with either a handsaw or power saw. Handsaws are generally used for a limited number of cuts or to finish off circular saw cuts. Power saws equipped with a crosscut or combination carbide-tipped blade are faster, more accurate, and produce cleaner cuts than handsaws and should be used if you have a lot of cuts to make. A circular saw is the most versatile saw and can be used for crosscutting as well as ripping (below). As with all cutting operations, make sure you wear safety glasses and hearing protection and that your work is well supported on saw horses or some other stable surface.

RIPPING *Ripping wood* is cutting along its length, with the grain, and is done with a handsaw or power saw. Handsaws especially made for ripping are available, but you can probably get by with just a crosscut saw. The wood you're going to use for a job should be the proper width, and therefore the amount of ripping you'll have to do will be minimal. If you need to rip a lot of boards or want an edge that's straight and true, however, then the table saw is the tool of choice.

A high-quality blade produces superior results and reduces the tendency of the saw or wood to bind or kick back.

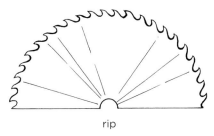
rip

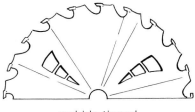
carbide-tipped
combination blade

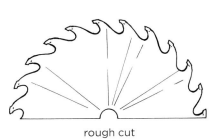
rough cut

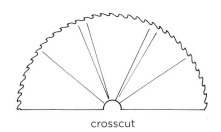
crosscut

A half-lap joint is created with a circular saw and a wood chisel and is used to connect two timbers. ▪

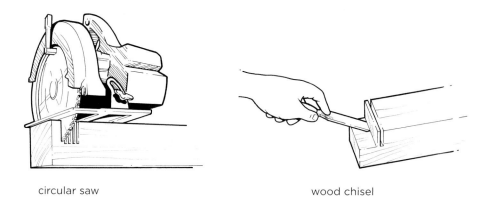

circular saw   wood chisel

NOTCHING Notching provides a way to support one piece of wood on another or to connect two pieces of wood. The basic notch is made by cutting a corner out of the end of a piece of lumber, as in the posts in the joisted footbridge (see page 189). Small notches can be made with a handsaw, while a circular saw makes quick work of larger, more numerous notches. Measure the depth and length of the notch and mark it off with a small square. Make the cuts, first across the board and then up from the end.

A more sophisticated notch, used to connect two timbers, is the half-lap joint, which is typically created with a circular saw and wood chisel. Mark the length of the half-lap using a square and set your saw blade to the depth of the cut. Cut at the line first and work your way to the end by making multiple cuts about ⅜ inch apart. Then position your chisel and strike the end with a hammer or wooden mallet to remove the remaining wood and finish the notch.

▪ Making Connections

The methods and materials used to connect and hold structures together are critically important and require time and attention as well as careful execution.

Fasteners

Whenever possible and appropriate, connections should be screwed or bolted together, not nailed; it's a more time-consuming approach, but it results in a stronger connection that can be easily undone in the event that changes or repairs are called for. Metal fasteners should be rust resistant: either galvanized, ceramic coated, or stainless steel. Galvanized fasteners come in two forms: hot dipped and electroplated. Hot-dipped nails hold better than electroplated, but the galvanized coating can pop off. Electroplated nails hold their coating, but over time tend to lose their grip on wood. Although they cost more, when it comes to rust resistance, stainless-steel screws are far superior to any coated fasteners, and I highly recommend them. Stainless steel is softer than other metals, however, so predrilling may be required. Decking screws with ceramic coatings are also available and cost less than stainless steel.

Although screws are clearly the preferred method for attaching decking to the frame, unless they are countersunk and plugged, they will be visible. If you'd rather have an "invisible" connection, there are a number of fastening systems used for decks, available at lumber and hardware stores, that would be appropriate for your bridge.

Drilling and Driving

When building paths, steps, and footbridges, drilling and driving go hand in glove. Drilling pilot holes makes screws easier to drive and reduces the possibility that a board will split from the outward pressure exerted by the screw. This is particularly true when a screw is installed near the end of a board. Choose a drill bit that is appropriate, usually the same diameter as the screw shaft. In instances where you want the head of the screw to be flush with the wood surface, use a countersinking bit.

Installing screws with a manual screwdriver is slow and tiring but, thankfully, has been made nearly obsolete by battery-operated drivers and drills. Drivers are specialized tools used mainly to install screws into gypsum board. Variable-speed drills or drills/drivers with adjustable torque settings are more appropriate for the projects in this book.

The type of driver bit that's needed depends on the screw head. Deck screws have two basic types of heads: Phillips and square. Phillips-head screws were a major improvement over the slotted-head screws, and the square-head screw improves on the Phillips. I find square heads hold the driver bit more securely, particularly in awkward positions, and are generally easier to use.

Unless you own a powerful drill/driver, lag screws are best installed using a socket wrench. A good pilot hole is essential for proper installation, and because lag screws are often under a lot of pressure, it's a good idea to use an appropriately sized washer to avoid crushing the surface of the wood.

Paths

4

ATHS ARE ROUTES of travel, ways for you to move from point A to point B and back again. They may lead to a main entrance, a backyard patio, or a secret hideaway. At their best, paths are also byways for the senses. You can enrich the path-traveling experience by incorporating elements that surprise and delight, such as colorful, fragrant flowers and the sounds of running water. This chapter explains how to create inviting, functional paths that will enhance your landscape. We begin with an overview of paths and some guiding principles, and then move on to specific projects.

What Paths Do

Paths connect the various parts of your landscape, making them more accessible. Strategically placed paths provide an organizational framework for your property by defining distinct areas and directing, with strong visual cues, where people should go. Good traffic flow is a hallmark of good design, and a well-thought-out network of footpaths can become the basis for a successful backyard landscape.

Delineating Paths

In interior design, walls, doors, and furniture placement define traffic patterns. Outdoors, paths are usually defined by features used in combination underfoot, on the sides, and overhead. When starting to plan your path, try to think in three dimensions. Imagine how you will feel as you move through space walking along the path.

What's Underfoot?

Whether bare earth that is compacted by constant use or an uninterrupted swath of cut stone, a path is first defined by what's underfoot. It's not surprising, then, that when designing paths we spend a great deal of time considering path materials and how to use them to best effect.

The bold, irregular flagstones in this simple path demand attention and direct walkers forward to the gate. ■

Relying solely on underfoot materials to define a path can be risky because walkers need compelling reasons not to stray. The path must clearly say, "Walk here and nowhere else." To encourage the walker to stay on a path, use materials that contrast sharply with the surrounding ground, and keep the path relatively short and direct so the destination is visible. If the journey is too long or the pull of the path weak, the walker is more likely to abandon it for a shortcut.

What's on the Sides?

The longer and more complex a path, the greater the need to direct and maintain a walker's attention. Providing clear edges and boundaries helps.

The simplest approach is to incorporate a border. Most borders tend to be subtle and are created by using narrow edging or by altering the orientation of the path's paving material. Using a different material, making it relatively wide, or setting it above the plane of the path makes the border more prominent.

Another approach is to use plantings as borders. Flowers, ground covers, low shrubs, and even small trees make excellent borders. Take time to choose plants that are appropriate for your particular situation. For example, choose low plants when you want to maintain a view, higher plants when you want to provide a screen or direct a view, and shade-loving plants for areas that don't receive much sun. When selecting planting materials, keep in mind that over time roots of larger trees and shrubs may invade paths, resulting in uneven surfaces and challenging walking conditions. If this possibility concerns you, ask your nursery supplier for advice and recommendations.

A fence or wall makes a solid border. If you already have fences and walls on your property, consider laying out your path to take advantage of them. You can also build low walls to border your path.

Let function and location guide your choice of border style. For example, use a low split-rail fence in a rural setting, a tall stockade-type fence as a privacy screen in a suburban landscape, a low stone wall to define a path running through a field, or a retaining wall to define a path at the toe of a slope. If there are steep drop-offs on your property, install a fence or dense plantings at their edges as a safety measure.

Lush plantings clearly define a path but take time to fill in and mature. To create a border on a budget, first define the edges of the path, then gradually expand the border each season by adding plants. ▪

A pergola defines a path on the sides and top, but a well-placed trellis can be an equally effective tool.

What's Overhead?

Paths can be defined effectively, and sometimes dramatically, by what's overhead. Trees provide a natural canopy. Some trees are towering and majestic; others are low and sheltering. One of my favorite paths runs along the edge of our pond; the low, overhanging hemlock boughs define and shelter the path. It takes many years for trees to grow tall enough to create a canopy, so new paths are usually designed to take advantage of existing trees.

Another option is to construct an instant canopy with a trellis or pergola; both provide excellent support for climbing vines. Dappled light and fragrant blooms make strolling beneath these structures a magical experience.

Consider the Setting

In the planning stages of your project (see chapter 2), you documented the physical features of your home and landscape. This step allows you to understand and respect the raw materials you have to work with. Although some of history's finest architectural and garden designs — the cliff and adobe dwellings of the Southwest Native Americans and the Japanese stroll gardens, for example — are notable for being in tune with their natural surroundings, most of us are all too eager to impose our will on the landscape rather than being sensitive and responsive to it. Strive to work with the landscape, not against it. Your paths will be most successful if you first carefully observe the existing landscape and then follow its lead.

Look for Opportunities

A good way to tune in to the landscape is to look for opportunities when you encounter problems or obstacles. Topographical features, for example, can help define and direct a path. If you encounter a steep incline, large rock, or ledge outcropping as you lay out your path, look for ways to incorporate it into your design. The same is true with vegetation. Resist the impulse to rip out that tangled briar patch that seems to be in the way. Instead, take time to assess the plants, then consider removing only some of them and adding plants to complement what remains.

During the early planning stages for the path on the west side of my house, for example, I knew that the pond-side, sloping edge would need to be well defined. Thoroughly enamored with the mountain laurel's beautiful white flowers and year-round foliage, I initially considered removing everything but that. But after speaking with a plant expert, I learned that the witch hazel, which was interspersed with the mountain laurel, should stay. Not only did its foliage contrast nicely with that of the laurel, but it also had a complementary branch structure and would provide additional color in late fall.

Make Allowances for the Climate

In the early planning stages, be sure to consider and make allowances for the regional climate and your property's microclimate. If you live in a hot, dry area, plan for shade and use materials that don't absorb heat. If a path will cross an open area subject to wind and drifting snow, include a windbreak — either plants or a fence — in your design. In rainy areas, choose materials that are rot resistant and provide solid footing when wet, and be sure to provide drainage for areas of the path where water tends to collect.

Establish a Path Hierarchy

Even small yards benefit from more than a single path. For example, one path might travel from the driveway or street to the front door, another from the garage to the side door, and possibly a third from the back door to a garden or a shed. Even though you may want to create just one path now, it's a good idea to think about your future needs.

Before you start to work on the design of your path, make a preliminary list of all the paths you might want to create. Identify each path's purpose, how it will be used, and where it will be located, and then rank the paths in order of importance. Review any notes you made on sensory impressions (see page 32), then walk through your property with each path in mind.

The following questions will help you refine the path hierarchy:

- *What areas of your property do you need or want to access?*
- *Which paths will be used most frequently?*
- *Who will be using the paths (members of the household, pets, friends, guests, delivery people)?*
- *What, if anything, will these people be carrying (groceries, packages, tools, children)?*
- *Will the path need to accommodate strollers or wheelchairs?*
- *Which paths will be easy to locate because their beginnings and ends are clearly defined?*
- *Which paths will have flexible locations or can meander because they are less constrained by function or destination?*

Put It on Paper

At this point your designs are preliminary; draw them on tracing paper placed over the site plan you prepared in chapter 2. Draw primary paths first, using the reference points on your site plan to help with placement. Primary paths should be relatively easy to locate, because they are used most often. Next, sketch in the more discretionary secondary paths. These are meant to be basic drawings, so use simple lines.

Choose a Style

Begin developing your paths by determining their style. Look to your surroundings for direction and take your first cues from your house. Is it formal or informal, modern or traditional, rough or refined, simple or complex? Generally, it's a good idea to be consistent.

What about the yard and landscape? Is your property varied, with lawn, fields, and woodlands? Is everything neat and manicured, or does the grass get high and plantings weedy every now and then? As you plan, be mindful that it takes time to keep a property well groomed, so be realistic about how much time you're willing to devote to maintenance.

As a general rule, paths near the house should be somewhat formal, and paths that venture into the wilds of your property less formal. Rules can be broken, of course, and there is no better reason to break them than to satisfy your personal taste. You want to be pleased with the results, so your preferences should inform your decisions.

The material you choose to put underfoot and how you install it also have significant impact on style. For example, cut stone, such as regular flagstone, has a formal appearance and wood rounds an informal appearance, but each can be installed in a manner that will achieve the opposite effect.

Establish the Form

"Form follows function" is a good design principle except that it tends to be overly simplistic. The form of your paths should follow their function, but *function* in this context suggests that utility is more important than aesthetics. A path's function is never strictly utilitarian, so it should integrate the aesthetic as well as the practical.

Shape

The initial aspect of form to consider is shape: how the paths will be laid out on the land. As explained by Christopher Alexander and colleagues in *A Pattern Language: Towns, Buildings, Construction*, successful paths should follow human preferences:

> The layout of paths will seem right and comfortable only when it is compatible with the process of walking. . . . As you walk along you scan the landscape for intermediate destinations. . . . You try . . . to walk in a straight line toward these points. This naturally has the effect that you will cut corners and take "diagonal" paths, since these are the ones which often form straight lines between your present position and the point which your are making for. . . . To lay out paths, first place goals at natural points of interest. Then connect the goals to one another to form the paths. (New York: Oxford University Press, 1977, 586–88)

People do tend to walk in a straight line, but the important point is that you can guide people by using goals, or "points." Used here, *goal*

Work with your topography, not against it, always looking for creative solutions. Designing this path to curve gently around the large rock and trees adds character and interest.

means something slightly different than a final destination. Think of goals as intermediate destinations, focal points for the journey that beckon you forward.

To get an initial sense of the shape of your path, take a walk. Try different routes, being sure to entertain options that you might first consider unlikely or even out of the question. Sketch them as individual overlays to your plan and note the differences. Which route is the easiest to negotiate? Is the most obvious path really the route you want people to take? Is there something that you want to lead people to or past? How would that shape your path?

The topography of your property will most likely play a role in shaping the path. Here is a perfect place to practice that turning-problems-into-opportunities attitude. What if a big rock or tree is right where you want to run your path? A gentle curve will not only avoid the problem but will also add character to your path. Is that slope too short and steep for a set of stairs? Try laying out a path that rises up along the slope and incorporates a switchback that brings you to the top and then back to where you started. If you think positively, you can come up with creative solutions that work and feel right because they respond to the natural surroundings.

Width

The width of a path depends on how it's going to be used. Obviously, a path meant to guide people single file doesn't have to be as wide as one on which two people will stroll hand in hand. You'll need less space in a garden path if you're only carrying a shovel and more space if you want to push a wheelbarrow loaded with tools.

Explore Your Options

Consider a hypothetical path from a driveway to the front door. A typical arrangement might have the front door facing the street with the driveway to one side. A straight path would be a diagonal directly from the driveway to the front door. While this tack is certainly the most efficient route, it's not very pleasing because the angle of access to the house is awkward and abrupt.

A better solution would be to walk along the path until you are nearly opposite the front door, then to gradually turn and move toward the door. This approach keeps you away from the house so that you can appreciate and view the space you're entering. But a path traveling through an open lawn might appear arbitrary, feel uncomfortable, and be subject to short-cuts. To remedy this, introduce a goal, such as an eye-catching plant or sculpture. By placing a goal at the end of the first "leg" and then subtly directing the walker's attention to the destination — the front door — the path will feel natural and comfortable.

People routinely cut corners while walking a path. Therefore, use 90-degree turns sparingly and in only the most formal situations, such as entryways to homes and in formal gardens. If you use a 90-degree turn, you can make it feel more natural and reduce the desire to cut the corner by providing a strong goal at the inter-section and screening the destination with plantings or perhaps a low fence.

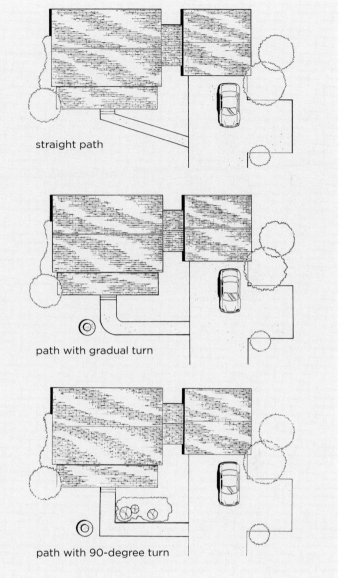

straight path

path with gradual turn

path with 90-degree turn

The width of a path does not have to remain constant; it can vary to match changing requirements. For example, the house-side approach to my bridge traverses a steep embankment. A single-file path seems appro-priate here. However, to encourage people to walk together, the stairs leading to my bridge and the bridge itself are wide enough for two people to walk side by side. To keep them walking together, the path leading away is wider than the bridge for about 30 feet, then it splits into two narrower paths, each of which has a different destination; these are more suitable for single-file travel.

In addition to changing width along its length, a path can also mean-der. Perhaps rather than totally circumventing that big rock, you'd like to call attention to its interesting color or unique shape. If so, allow the path to approach the rock, then snake around it. If you want to be able to turn a wheelbarrow around without trampling plantings, plan a path of at least 4-foot width so that you'll have enough room to do so.

Path widths and uses

MINIMUM WIDTH	MATERIAL	USE
12"–18"	Small, widely spaced stepping-stone path	Single file, slow pace with attention down toward the feet
18"–2'	Trodden-earth, grass, large and closely spaced stepping-stones, solid, and loose-fill paths	Single file, quicker pace with attention on surroundings
3'–4'	Trodden-earth, grass, solid or loose-fill paths	One person pushing a wheelbarrow or carrying a trash can
4'–5'	Trodden-earth, grass, solid or loose-fill paths	Two people walking abreast

▇ Orchestrate a Dynamic Experience

A dynamic experience is perhaps the most critical aspect of path design and what distinguishes an exceptional path from a purely functional one. The direction and speed of travel, framed views, and elements of mystery and surprise all contribute to a dynamic experience.

As you plan, fine-tune the shape and width of your paths and incorporate features such as entrances, goals, and transitions. Keep in mind that a path's purpose, use, and length necessarily influence its design. A short, mainly utilitarian path should be simple and straightforward, whereas a garden or strolling path is more interactive and needs more complexity to engage the walker.

Formal stone pillars clearly mark the entrance to this property. Because of their size, the short stone walls that define the edges of the path don't compete for our attention. ▇

Incorporating a goal, such as a gazing ball, in a path will hold a walker's attention and urge her forward. Goals also make excellent points of transition at turns and intersections. ▪

Beginnings

Every path needs an entrance. Entrances don't have to be monumental, but they should provide a clear sense of welcome and arrival. A clearly defined entrance heightens the sense of separation between areas. Entrances can be defined subtly, by introducing a change in walking surface, or obviously, by placing markers such as large rocks, stone pillars, and wood posts on either side of the path. A more dramatic sense of entry can be created with an opening in a fence or wall, a gate, columns, or a pergola.

Goals

Goals urge walkers forward and hold their attention, contributing significantly to the dynamic experience of a path. Make the first goal visible soon after crossing the threshold. This doesn't necessarily mean that the path has to lead straight to the goal, but the goal should lie within the line of sight or awareness.

An effective way to introduce drama and mystery into a path is a technique called "conceal and reveal." First show a goal, then screen it with plantings or fencing. Consider the length and shape of the path, then space and situate goals to best advantage to urge walkers forward.

Goals take many forms. They may already exist in the landscape — a favorite tree or unusual rock outcropping, for example. Or they may be "imported"; statues, sculpture, plantings, and garden ornaments all make excellent goals. When used judiciously as motivators to direct the eye, such ornaments appear necessary and purposeful, not arbitrary or overdone. Goals don't always have to be visible; they can also appeal to the senses of hearing and smell. The sound of trickling water and melodic chimes and the scent of fragrant flowers are powerful goals.

This inviting retreat is the perfect place to enjoy a refreshing glass of iced tea or lemonade on a hot summer day. ▪

Places of Rest or Refuge

Places of rest or refuge play a special role in path design; they offer respite from the hectic pace of life and are havens for quiet contemplation. Situate seats, benches, or swings in alcoves or bump-outs along a path to take advantage of a view or to provide a private retreat. A clearing in a wooded area with seating along an edge or a gazebo in the middle makes a wonderful refuge, as does an arbor with built-in seating. Both offer a sense of shelter and protection.

Transitions

A path might travel from a formal area near the house, to a less formal flower garden, through an informal vegetable garden, and finally to woodlands at the edge of your property. To echo this journey, punctuate the path with transitions from formal to informal, refined to rough, and wide to narrow. These transitions function as secondary entrances and make the experience more dynamic.

The key to creating an effective transition is clarity: make the change obvious. One approach is to alter the way the path material is installed or to change the paving material at each point of transition. But if this technique proves too subtle, reinforce it by introducing something on the side of the path or overhead. For example, a Y-intersection where a primary path branches off to a secondary path might be articulated with a change in the type and spacing of the path material as well as by using markers similar to, but perhaps smaller than, what was used at the path entrance.

If you want a path to narrow as it enters a wooded area, visual cues can alert the walker to the change. For example, as the path along my house leaves the open area and prepares to head into the woods and down to the bridge, mountain laurel pinches in the path on either side.

Transitions often occur at changes in elevation. For safety's sake, mark these points with something decorative and easy to see, such as a post-and-rope railing or a wooden archway. Shallow steps are easily overlooked, so make them obvious for walkers.

Signal transitions by altering the width of the path *(A)*, the pattern of installation *(B)*, or the material *(C)*.

A

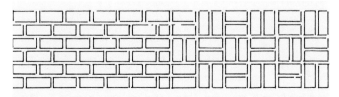

B

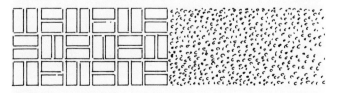

C

■ **Use switchbacks or sharp curves.** Doubling back or introducing a sharp bend will lengthen the journey physically and also make it feel longer by shifting the focus and hiding a portion of the path.

■ **Use materials that slow the speed of travel.** Small stepping-stones with wide spaces between them require strict attention, slowing the walker and making the path seem longer.

■ **Give walkers cause to pause.** Flowering plants, garden sculptures, and places to sit all encourage walkers to stop, admire, and rest.

■ **Vary width.** A path that starts wide and gradually narrows appears longer than it is.

■ **Use contrasting colors.** Light-colored objects call attention to themselves and appear close, while dark colors recede. If used at the beginning and end of a path, respectively, they give the path an illusion of length.

Controlling Speed

Varying the pace and rhythm of a path also enriches the experience. Do this for variety alone if you must, but it's usually better to do it for a reason. For example, slow the pace to call attention to a special plant or statue. Then hasten the pace to rush someone by a less-than-attractive part of your landscape, such as a compost pile.

There are many ways to influence speed. Slow pedestrians down by changing from a solid surface to loose-fill material. Adjusting the size of stepping-stones — larger ones for faster movement, smaller ones for slower — is an easy way to control speed. Even the installation pattern can provide an element of control. Installing brick pavers lengthwise in the direction of travel draws the eye forward and encourages a quicker pace, for example, whereas turning them 90 degrees has the opposite effect.

You can also control walking speed by manipulating shape. People naturally move faster in a straight line than they do when negotiating a curve, and they tend to slow down as a path narrows. If incorporating curves to control speed, don't use them arbitrarily, and keep the principles of good design in mind; your path shouldn't mimic a grand-prix racing circuit. Width is a little more difficult to abuse, but, again, use changes in width purposefully and judiciously.

Directing the Eye and Framing Views

While a path's principal purpose is foot travel, an important secondary purpose is to give the eyes avenues for exploration. You might want to showcase a nearby garden planting or direct attention to a favorite view. Think about what captures your attention, turns your head, or holds your gaze as you walk, then try to incorporate some of these features into your design.

Paths of widely spaced or small stepping-stones force walkers to literally watch their steps, whereas solid paths or paths with larger stepping-stones allow greater freedom to look around. You can combine these two patterns to draw the walker, head down, past something you don't want her to see and then release her attention in time to admire a lovely view.

Curves are an excellent way to direct the eyes. People tend to focus on the ground when negotiating a curve, then look up and ahead as the path straightens. At the end of a curve, reward walkers with an interesting focal point or view.

Japanese-garden designers are renowned for their skill in framing distant views. Instead of revealing a body of water, house, or other structure all at once, for example, they do it gradually, teasing the eyes by directing our gaze through plantings or trees.

Surprise and Intrigue

Japanese-garden designers are also masters of surprise and intrigue, a design technique that leads walkers in alternating tangents, first left and then right, to open and reveal new vistas or different aspects of the same view. Along the way, strategically placed plantings may first conceal and then reveal points of interest.

Refine Your Design

Develop the design of your path by incorporating some or all of the elements described above, experimenting with each on a different overlay and incorporating the ones you want to use on a final plan. As you work the design on paper, you might want to step outside and roughly lay out the path to get a better sense of how it will work on your property.

When you feel that you've done all you can do, set aside the plan for a few days. When you come back to it, look at it critically, evaluating it for details you might have overlooked. Are there problems or omissions that you need to address? Also, read through the construction section for each type of path to make sure you're considering a path that's appropriate for your situation. When you're satisfied with the plan, you're ready to enter the construction phase.

Path-Building Basics

Although each type of path has unique construction techniques and requirements, a number of issues apply to all paths. Familiarize yourself with these and refer to them as you begin constructing of your path.

Locate the Path

Laying out your design on the ground helps you visualize the plan in greater detail. Start by locating the path relative to the reference points you noted in your site plan, such as the house, driveway, or other permanent structure. Establish one side of a path and then lay out the second side relative to it. Mark the edges with wood stakes, marking paint, a garden hose, or granulated lime.

STRAIGHT LINES Lay out lines that need to be perfectly straight and parallel, such as those required for the installation of pavers and cut stone, with

When laying out a straight path, set stakes at the beginning and at the end and pull strings between them. If necessary, add a few intermediate stakes. Measure to be sure width is consistent.

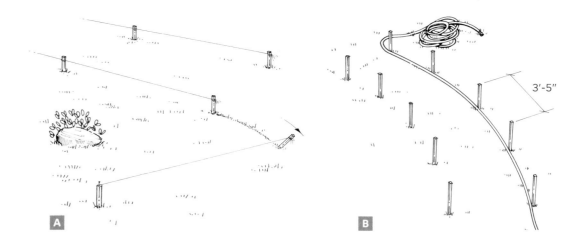

Create curves using stakes and string *(A)* or a garden hose *(B)*. When designing a curve, strive to create one that is pleasing to the eye. ▪

taut string that is stretched between stakes. Use a tape measure or a piece of wood, cut to length, to ensure a consistent width. To facilitate excavation and site preparation, establish the layout line 6 to 12 inches outside the actual width.

CURVED LINES Lay out curves using string and stakes or a garden hose. To create a perfect arc or circle, set a stake at the center point. Attach a string of appropriate length to the center stake, then pull the string taut. Hold the end of the string in your hand with a stick or other sharp implement, then scribe the ground, keeping the string taut as you move around the center stake.

A flexible garden hose is the best tool for laying out broad or compound curves. Once your starting point is established, lay out the hose along the path you expect the curve to take. Mark and double-check curves by driving 3-foot stakes into the ground every few feet and sighting along them. Make any needed adjustments now.

Accommodate the Terrain

Once the layout of your path is set, it's time to attend to the "lay of the land." First assess the effects of any slopes on your path. A pitch greater than 2 inches of rise for 12 inches of run (2/12) is approaching a slope of 10 percent, which is steep for a path and raises concerns about safety and runoff. Steep sections can be managed either by incorporating a couple of steps or by adjusting the grade by excavating the steep portion and installing a retaining wall. If your path is steep over a long span, consider rerouting it. The following chart will help you determine what terrain-altering measures you might have to take.

Evaluating slope

SLOPE (%)	RUN (inches per foot)	DESCRIPTION
0–1.5	0–³⁄₁₆	Relatively flat; may require the installation of drainage to keep from flooding
1.5–5	³⁄₁₆–⁵⁄₈	Excellent slope for paths; requires little adjustment
5–8	⁵⁄₈–1	An 8 percent slope qualifies as a ramp; consider adding steps
8–15	1–1⁷⁄₈	Steep for a path; may be slippery when wet and icy, and loose materials may wash away
15 and greater	1⁷⁄₈ or more	Stairs, not a path, would be best for this slope

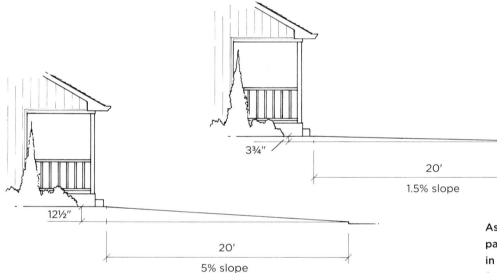

3¾"

20'

1.5% slope

12½"

20'

5% slope

As you begin to lay out your path, determine its slope. A slope in the 1.5% to 5% range is ideal for a path. A slope of greater than 5% may be better served by a ramp or steps.

If your path runs parallel to the house or another structure, build a slight cross-pitch — that is, a slight pitch across the width of the path — of about ¼ inch per foot, to encourage water to run off and away from the house.

While paths that curve back and forth are pleasing to the eye, paths that undulate sharply up and down are not. To smooth things out, fill low spots with free-draining material such as crushed gravel topped with sand. Assuming there are no large rocks or ledge in the way, shave off any high spots, but resist the temptation to use the removed material to fill in low spots; doing so would probably result in drainage problems. Removing lots of material sometimes necessitates the construction of a retaining wall; it's often possible to avoid this by focusing your energy filling rather than on digging.

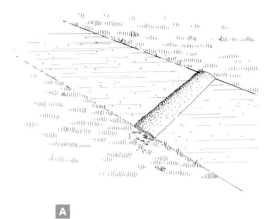

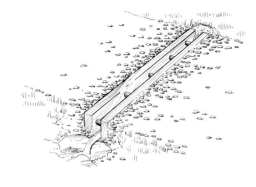

Water bars *(A)* and water breaks *(B)* help control surface erosion and are most often used in loose-fill paths. It's not always possible to predict where erosion will occur, so use these when the need arises.

CAUTION!

Before you dig, be absolutely certain there are no buried pipes or wires in the area to be cleared. If you will be digging down a foot or more, contact your local utilities to find out the name of the company in your area that is charged with locating and marking underground utilities. For more information, see page 33.

Installing water bars or breaks on the surface of the path helps to control surface erosion. A water bar is a small rise that directs the water to the side of the path, whereas a water break is a small trench or shallow swale cut into the path. Both stop water from running down the length of a path and eroding it.

Prepare a Materials List

Before you begin construction of your path, prepare a complete list of the materials you need for the project. Use your plans and enlist the help of suppliers. Also use the tips on estimating included with the construction information later in this chapter.

Clear the Ground

In most cases, you'll need to prepare the ground before starting to work on your path. Typically, you'll clear a wide swath for grass, loose-fill, and solid paths and do only spot clearing for a stepping-stone path.

SOD Removing grass and sod is by far the easiest clearing task. After the path is laid out, cut grass and sod with an edger, peel it back with a square-nosed shovel, roll it up, and carry it away in a wheelbarrow. You might want to save some pieces to use to fill in around the finished path; if not, give it away or compost it.

ROOTS Cut small tree and shrub roots with the sharp blade of a shovel; larger ones may require an ax. Before you remove any roots, however, do a little research: once a root is cut, it's cut forever. Consult an expert before cutting through more than 25 percent of a plant's surface roots. Although small roots may appear inconsequential, some plants are invasive and can wreak havoc with a path, particularly one constructed of solid materials.

ROCKS AND LEDGE If your path encounters rocks or ledge, first determine what can and cannot be removed. Large rocks are one thing, but boulders and ledge are quite another. Probe with a shovel or steel rod to reveal what you're dealing with. If it's something really big, you might need to consult an excavation contractor. Boulders can sometimes be removed with a backhoe or similar piece of equipment, and certain types of ledge can be cut away with a pneumatic jackhammer. In these situations, discretion is sometimes the better part of valor, however, and modifying the course of your path may be the wisest choice.

Prepare the Base

A base provides an appropriately stable "platform" for a path, isolating it from the effects of weather and the seasons, particularly winter freezing, moisture-induced swelling, and excessive summer drying. Some paths need little or no base preparation, while others require an extensive, deep base. Informal stepping-stone paths can roll with the punches, for example, whereas a solid path should always be level.

The goal of base building is to remove any material prone to swelling when it absorbs water and/or freezes, such as heavy soil and clay. Poor-draining material is replaced with material that compacts tightly and is free draining, such as crushed gravel, and may be topped with a leveling layer of sand on which stone or brick is placed. Base requirements vary depending on location and soil type. Guidelines for each path type are provided in the project instructions beginning on page 92.

Make Allowances for Proper Drainage

In the planning stage, you identified areas with potential drainage problems. Keep these in mind as you lay out your path. Avoiding poor drainage areas altogether is often the best way to deal with these locations, but that's not always possible. If your site is especially challenging, it might be wise to seek expert advice from a professional landscaper. Otherwise, you'll need to choose the most suitable path type and materials for the conditions. Another option is to elevate the path with a bridge or boardwalk (see chapter 6).

Keeping the path surface raised slightly above the surrounding ground is good practice generally: it helps safeguard the path from water damage. Building a slight crown into the base of loose-fill and solid paths also helps them to shed water, which is essential for any path built with long, level runs or in wet areas.

If the topography permits, bases in particularly poor draining soils may benefit from a perforated drainage pipe. Four-inch flexible or rigid plastic pipe that's used for drains in house foundation footings works

Types of Edging Materials

■ **Stone.** Many kinds of stone can be used for edgings: rounded fieldstone that's found on-site and simply laid on top of the ground; blasted or quarried stone that's split into thin pieces and installed on edge, partially buried; and pieces of cut stone or recycled cobblestone.

■ **Masonry.** Brick and concrete pavers, often installed on end in "soldier" or "toothed" patterns, make effective edges. Manufacturers of concrete pavers make a wide array of decorative edgings in straight, angled, and curved profiles, as well as curb blocks intended to hold other pavers in place.

■ **Metal and plastic.** Typically, these types of edgings are used when you don't want the edging to be visible. Both are available in varying gauges, or thicknesses, and lengths. Heavy-duty materials are worth any extra expense: they are easier to install and last longer. Specialty vinyl edges are available for brick and masonry pavers and help hold the pavers in place.

■ **Wood.** Because it will be exposed to moisture, soil, and the elements, wood is not the best choice for this type of application. I consider it a last resort. Wood boards, such as 1×4s and 4×4 or 4×6 landscaping timbers, can be successfully used for edging but they must be a rot-resistant species or pressure treated. Composite timbers look like wood but don't rot.

Set 1×4s or 2×6s on edge and partially buried; 4×4s and 4×6s can be installed directly on the ground or partially buried.

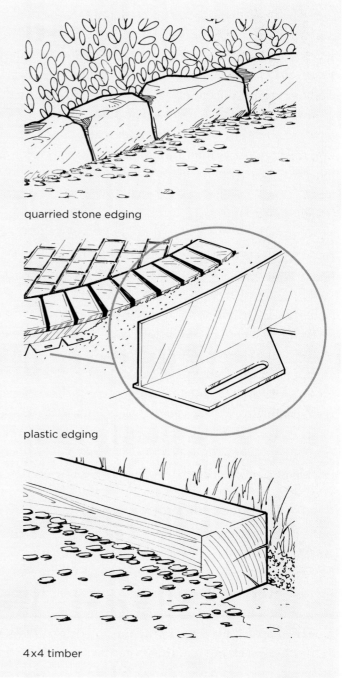

quarried stone edging

plastic edging

4×4 timber

well for this purpose and is available at building-supply stores. Install it perforations down, on top of the base layer of crushed stone or processed gravel, so it spans the entire length of the wet area. Pitch it down toward a spot, if there is one, where the water can drain to daylight, and install a 90-degree elbow and short length of pipe to carry water away from the path. To keep the pipe from becoming clogged with sediment, wrap it with filter fabric or select a pipe that is made with an integral "sock."

Consider Edging

Edgings create a distinct border for the path, stabilize path material by keeping it in place, and prevent the surrounding ground from encroaching on the path. They are also decorative. Stone, masonry, metal, plastic, and wood all make effective edgings. With edgings, virtually anything goes, so be creative while keeping the style of the path in mind. If you want a subtle edge for a serene pea-stone path, for example, jagged blasted stone might not be the best choice.

Edgings for loose-fill paths are usually installed before the path material, whereas those for solid paths are typically installed as the path is laid down. Unless a manufacturer specifies otherwise, install edging on the same base material as the finished path. This way, if there is any movement, the edging will move with the path. If the edging you're using is relatively wide, increase the width of the base accordingly.

Edging height, if not predetermined by type, is one of the most important decisions you'll make when installing edging. This is both an aesthetic and a maintenance issue, particularly if the path is surrounded by lawn. If the edging is lower than the blade of your lawn mower, you'll be able to mow over it with no problem; if not, be prepared for lots of tedious trimming. On the other hand, if the edging is set too low, it may not do its job very well. Optimum edging height balances function and maintenance.

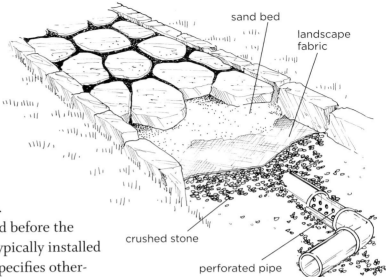

Perforated drainage pipe is useful where soil drains poorly. To prevent sand from infiltrating the crushed stone, install landscape fabric between the sand and stone.

Constructing Your Path

First decide which path type is most suitable for your purpose. Read the opening descriptions and appropriate uses for each path type before making a decision. Once you've made a selection but before you begin working, read about the project so you understand what's required, then gather the necessary tools and materials.

TRODDEN-EARTH PATHS

Trodden-earth paths, or dirt paths, are the simplest and most primitive path type. Worn into the ground by countless generations, they provide physical evidence of human and animal activity and of the perpetual need to get from here to there. Dirt paths have led farmers to barns and cows to pasture. They are the shortcuts we took as children to and from the bus stop, a friend's house, or a secret hideout.

Natural paths are worn into the ground over time with regular use, but letting a path form this way can take years. You can make a natural-looking dirt path in hours or days by following these simple instructions.

Appropriate Uses

A dirt path works well in vegetable and flower gardens; through dew-dampened fields and woodlands; and as a casual route to a playhouse, tree house, or neighbor's yard.

Site Preparation

After laying out the path (see page 85), clear the ground of potential toe-stubbing and ankle-twisting hazards, such as large rocks. If the path passes through underbrush or low-hanging branches, make way for the walker by removing anything that might scratch bare legs, knock a hat off a head, or spring back and hit someone.

Preparing the Base

Because the soil is the path surface, dirt paths require little, if any, base preparation. However, it's important that the earth beneath a dirt path drain well; sandy soils are best. If you've noticed that the path area is often wet or soggy, remove some of the subsoil and replace it with crushed gravel to improve drainage.

Unsuitable soils should be removed to a depth of 2 to 3 inches. If you're creating a sunken path to mimic the look of an old dirt path, simply clear unsuitable materials to a depth of 2 to 3 inches below the desired finish height.

If the soil already drains well, probe for rocks and roots just beneath the surface that might be exposed as the path is used and remove them. Then level any bumps and dips.

Edging

Dirt paths are meant to be informal and so don't need any edging. If you want to add visual interest along the path, consider planting a border of flowers or shrubs.

Installing Finish Material

In a trodden-earth path, the soil is the finish material. If you removed poor-draining soil when preparing the base, you'll want to add the new soil to the proper depth now. You can also use it to help level any bumps or dips. Firmly pack the soil with a hand tamper.

Even if soil drains well, during rainy periods dirt paths sometimes turn into mud baths; this is particularly true for sunken paths. To help minimize puddling and promote good drainage, fill in any low spots so the path is level. Build up the path so it crowns in the middle, causing water to run off to the sides. Also consider installing landscape fabric and perforated pipe to improve drainage (see illustration on page 91).

Maintenance

To maintain a trodden-earth path, follow this rule first and foremost: use it or lose it. If you don't, Mother Nature will quickly reclaim the path. From time to time, you also may need to remove rocks and roots and top off the path with soil. A path that's worn and uneven has charm and character but can be a hazard for walkers. Keeping the path level will help ensure walker comfort and safety.

GRASS PATHS

Grass is lush, inviting, and soft. Grass paths seem close kin to trodden-earth paths, but they didn't originate until the nineteenth century, when they were artfully used in formal English gardens, long symbols of wealth and privilege. While they still tend to be somewhat formal, grass paths can provide a seamless link between a lawn and other parts of your property.

With the advent of sophisticated seed mixtures, fertilizers, and power mowers, grass has become a ubiquitous part of the contemporary home landscape. But a large expanse of lawn can be costly to install and maintain: so much so, in fact, that many homeowners are now replacing significant portions of their lawns with planting beds and ground covers. If you want to minimize your maintenance chores but don't want to remove the lawn completely, consider reducing the lawn to path width in some areas. Grass paths offer all the benefits of turf at minimum investment, creating inviting walkways and beautifying the landscape.

Grass paths are the most site-sensitive of all the paths, so before you decide to create a grass path, determine whether the conditions bode well for its success. Lawn grasses thrive in sunny locations, and they require ample moisture and fertile soil. Grasses are bred for less-than-optimum conditions, but these grass types have specific needs, which may be difficult to meet. Check with a local nursery, and research grasses available by mail via catalogs and the Internet.

If you live in a drought-prone area, a grass path is not a good idea. Grass requires relatively large quantities of water to remain in tip-top shape.

Appropriate Uses

A grass path is best used in low-traffic areas that link sections of lawns or gardens, as a walkway through a flower garden or from a deck or patio to a backyard gazebo, or as a shortcut through a field or meadow. Grass paths do not tolerate heavy use, and if you're not careful, they may devolve into trodden-earth paths. When a grass path is wet, expect soaking shoes and wet feet.

Site and Soil Preparation

Whether you're planting grass seed or installing sod, site and soil preparation is basically the same. After you've laid out the path (see page 85), clear the area of any unwanted vegetation, rocks, and surface roots. Rake the ground smooth, leveling any bumps and dips.

Next, check the depth and quality of the topsoil. To thrive, grass requires about 4 inches of fertile topsoil. Dig a few small test holes in various locations along the path to see how deep the topsoil is. Then, test the soil for pH and nutrient levels. You can do the test yourself using a kit purchased from a garden-supply store or nursery, or you can take a soil sample and send it to your state Cooperative Extension Service for analysis. The latter approach, which takes about a week to 10 days, may be more expensive, but the results are usually more accurate and informative. With the test results and recommendations in hand, you're ready to adjust the soil.

Unless the soil is unusually fertile, it's probably a good idea to begin by adding a layer of organic matter, such as well-aged manure or compost. Then add a natural fertilizer blend that matches the soil-test recommendations. Till the organic matter and fertilizer 4 to 6 inches into the ground. Let the soil sit for at least a week, then give it a good watering unless it has been well soaked by rainfall.

If the soil's pH is lower than 6.5, add granulated or pelletized limestone; if the pH is higher than 7.5, add powdered sulfur. The soil test will indicate the right amount to use for your soil. Till the soil again and rake the surface smooth.

Installing Finish Material

Choosing the right grass for your path is very important. Although there are thousands of varieties of grasses, there are only about a dozen that are suitable for lawns and paths. They're broken down into two broad categories, cool-season and warm-season grasses.

Cool-season grasses are commonly used in northern climates and grow best in spring or fall, when temperatures are between 60°F and 75°F. Warm-season grasses thrive when the temperatures are between 80°F and 95°F and do best in southern climates.

SOWING SEED

Sowing seed on prepared ground is the least expensive way to create a grass path, and it may be the only way to get the exact grass variety you'd

Types of Grasses

The following grasses are grouped by climate. All these grasses will do well in optimal conditions, but some meet certain challenges better than others. Seeds are often blended to create mixes that take advantage of the best characteristics of each. Be sure to check with a local expert at a garden-supply center, nursery, or the Cooperative Extension Service before deciding which grass to buy.

COOL-SEASON GRASSES

■ **Bluegrass** (*Poa* spp.). Fine-bladed grass that requires a lot of water and fertilizing to stay in peak condition; needs light, well-drained soil, full sun, and doesn't tolerate heavy traffic.

■ **Creeping red fescue** (*Festuca rubra*). Adapts to many soil conditions; prefers full sun but tolerates some shade; does not stand up to heavy traffic.

■ **Tall fescue** (*Festuca* spp.). Deep roots make it drought resistant and excellent for erosion control if you are planning a path on a slope or hill; grows well in most soils and is more tolerant of periodic drought than most cool-season grasses; can be grown in full sun and light shade; stands up to heavy traffic.

■ **Perennial ryegrass** (*Lolium perenne*). Sprouts quickly and is relatively pest and disease resistant; grows in a wide range of soils in full sun; stands up relatively well in high-traffic areas.

WARM-SEASON GRASSES

■ **Bermuda grass** (*Cynodon dactylon*). Prefers light-textured, well-drained, fertile soil and full sun; grows and spreads vigorously and needs to be contained with edgings and barriers; very heat, traffic, and drought tolerant, but turns brown fall through spring.

■ **Buffalo grass** (*Buchloe dactyloides*). Good choice for hot, dry regions; seldom needs irrigation water or fertilizing; prefers alkaline soils and grows well in full sun; stands up to heavy traffic.

■ **Blue gramma grass** (*Bouteloua gracilis*). Tough, disease- and drought-resistant, low-maintenance grass; prefers fertile, dry soil; grows well in full sun or light shade; stands up to heavy foot traffic.

■ **Zoysia** (*Zoysia* spp.). Very tough and drought resistant; benefits from yearly fertilization; prefers light-textured, well-drained soil; grows in full sun or light shade; slow-growing but requires less-frequent mowing; does well in high-traffic areas but turns brown with the first frost.

like to use. The trade-off is that it will be several weeks before the path can be walked on and longer still before it can be subjected to regular use. In northern cool-season climates, grass is best planted in late August to mid-September and also early to mid-spring. Weeds are less likely to compete with the grass seedlings if you sow in fall. In warm climates, sow seeds of warm-season grasses in late spring or early summer; sow seeds of cool-season grasses in mid-fall.

Spread the seed evenly along the path with a drop spreader, which puts the seed right where you want it at the recommended rate. Then gently rake the seed into the soil to a depth of about ¼ inch. It's important for grass to be in good contact with the soil. Rolling the path with a lightweight roller is helpful but not necessary. To keep the seed in place during rainstorms and to discourage birds from eating it, temporarily cover the area with cheesecloth until the seedlings get started, or mulch it lightly with weed-free straw. When the covering or mulch is in place, lightly water the seed. Keep the seedbed moist by sprinkling it lightly and frequently frequent until the seed germinates.

▲ Use a broadcast spreader in an overlapping, crisscross fashion to ensure even coverage over wide areas. ▪

INSTALLING SOD

Installing sod is the most expensive approach to making a grass path, but it has some advantages. Sod can be installed virtually any time during the growing season, it is not subject to being washed away or eaten, and once it is installed the path is essentially done, although it shouldn't be walked on for the first several weeks.

Sod is delivered in rolled strips, typically 1½ to 2 feet wide and 4 feet long, and can be purchased from a sod farm or garden-supply store. Plan to install the sod as soon as possible after it's delivered. In the meantime, keep it moist and shaded.

Install the sod lengthwise along the path, beginning at one edge with a full-length strip. Shorten the adjacent strip by cutting it in half with a large knife, and install it next to the first one in staggered fashion. Staggered planting minimizes the appearance of joints. If the soil is dry, moisten it before laying the sod, so the grass roots aren't robbed of their moisture when the sod is put down. Continue along the path, kneeling on a piece of plywood as you work to avoid crushing the newly installed sod. On steep slopes, use sod staples to temporarily hold the sod in place. When the installation is complete, tamp the sod into place with the head of a rake or roll it with a lightweight roller, then water enough for moisture to soak through the sod into the soil.

The critical time for new grass seed and sod is the first 3 to 4 weeks after planting. During this period, while the grass is establishing its roots, avoid walking on it and keep it evenly moist. Under unusually

▲ Ground should be smooth and level before installing sod. Butt pieces together snugly. ▪

dry or windy conditions, this might mean watering two or three times a day. Do not mow the grass until it is about 4 inches high, and even then trim it only an inch.

Edgings

Maintenance and aesthetics should be your top priorities when considering edging options for a grass path. A low-profile edging is subtle and keeps the path casual, whereas a prominent edging attracts the eye and formalizes the path.

A minimalist approach to edging can greatly reduce your maintenance chores. The first option would be to keep the path on the same plane as the surrounding ground and to use no edging. This allows you to easily mow the path and eliminates the need for some trimming, but leaves the path looking poorly defined.

One of the best low-profile options is thin metal or plastic edging. This type of edging keeps the path in shape, and if placed lower than your mower blade still allows you to mow the path easily with no trimming.

Heavier, more prominent edgings, such as a soldier course of red brick, contrast nicely with green grass and can produce an almost regal effect. Grass with this type of edging will have to be trimmed regularly with clippers or a power trimmer.

If you want a clean, crisp edge for your grass path, use brick.

Maintenance

While grass paths are the most maintenance-intensive of all the paths, you can take steps to minimize the amount of work required.

Mowing is the most regular maintenance chore. When you mow well-established grass, set the mower so that no more than one-third of the grass length is removed at one cutting. Using a mulching-type mower eliminates the need for raking or emptying a clipping bag and replenishes the soil with valuable nutrients.

To reduce the number of times that grass needs to be mowed, keep it a little on the long side; shorter grass tends to grow more quickly. Also, longer grass can shade out weeds. Optimal grass heights change with the growing season.

As a general rule, trim the grass to about 2 inches in the growing season and keep it at to 2¼ to 2½ inches during dry spells.

Once grass is well established, water it only when necessary. Excessive watering is wasteful and makes grass grow faster. Established grasses generally need about an inch of water per week during the growing season, although this varies somewhat with soil type, grass type, and weather conditions. When rainfall is insufficient, you will have to water the grass yourself. Morning watering is best; if it's done at midday, much of the water may evaporate, and evening watering can promote disease. Apply water slowly so that it can penetrate to at least 4 to 6 inches into the ground. Surface watering encourages development of roots that are shallow and weak.

Grass grown on well-prepared, fertile soil to which nutrient-rich clippings are regularly returned doesn't need much fertilizing. Test your soil periodically to determine what it needs, and follow recommendations. Chemical fertilizers are relatively inexpensive and readily available; however, they may not be the best choice for your grass path. Chemical fertilizers typically contain more of the required nutrients than natural or organic fertilizers, but they often release them (particularly nitrogen) so quickly that they induce growth spikes; if applied heavily, they can damage the grass. Fast-acting chemical fertilizers also can be harmful to earthworms and other beneficial soil organisms. Conversely, fertilizers made from natural materials — composted plants and manures, for instance — release nutrients slowly; many add soil-building organic matter and are earthworm-friendly.

Fall is the best time to fertilize cool-season grasses; the grass stores the nutrients over winter and releases them during the spring growing season. Fertilize warm-season grasses in spring when they are just beginning to grow; don't fertilize them in fall, as this encourages new growth when the grass should be slowing down in preparation for winter.

Weeds, insects, diseases, and rodents are just a few of the many threats to a grass path. By keeping the grass healthy, you significantly reduce the risk of problems occurring. If and when something does go wrong, ask yourself whether the path needs to be perfect before you rush to fix it. If you're not sure how to proceed, visit your local garden center for advice.

LOOSE-FILL PATHS

Loose-fill paths are evocative and can conjure cherished memories. They are cousins to trodden-earth and grass paths and keep walkers in close contact with the ground. The finish materials for loose-fill paths are dumped and spread, an approach quite different from that used in stepping-stone and solid paths, where the finish materials are carefully laid out and set by hand.

Loose-fill paths can be made with soft or hard materials, and the construction technique for each is similar. If soil conditions are favorable, you can install hard materials directly on the ground with little preparation. In contrast, soft materials usually need a proper base. In all cases, preparing a stable base that drains well will result in a more durable, functional path.

Appropriate Uses

Loose-fill paths work well in many settings. They make excellent walkways in a formal garden and are equally at home winding through a woodland setting. For obvious reasons, loose-fill paths are *not* appropriate for steep sites or in locations that must be regularly cleared of snow.

Soft Materials

Paths made with soft materials — such as pine needles, bark mulch, wood chips, and peanut shells — are informal and easy to construct. These lightweight, fibrous materials decompose rather quickly, however, and need to be replenished regularly. While this maintenance isn't difficult, be sure you want to commit to it long term before choosing this type of material. Soft materials offer little buffer from the ground, moisture, and dirt, and look most natural when allowed to encroach onto the surrounding ground, which they readily do.

For obvious reasons, soft materials should not be used in wet or boggy areas or in windy locations. If you prefer a well-defined path, plan to install an effective edging or consider using a hard material instead.

Hard Materials

Hard materials, such as washed stone, crushed stone, crushed shells, brick chips, and recycled glass, are heavy and don't decompose, making such paths easier to maintain once installed. A loose-fill path made of hard materials may be formal or informal.

Materials that compact well, such as crushed stones with the "fines" associated with processing, tend to blend in with the natural surroundings, giving a path a casual air. Compactable materials can be used successfully without a border. Washed or ornamental stones, on the other hand, do not compact and will spread if not kept in check by an appropriate edging.

Hard materials add another important dimension to a path — sound. The degree to which a material compacts affects the type of sound it makes. For example, shells and crushed stone that compacts well *crunch* underfoot, while round materials such as washed stone *click* underfoot.

To help tailor your path to your surroundings, choose locally available materials whenever possible. Here in landlocked western Massachusetts, for example, stone is a good choice, whereas a path made of crushed shells might seem strangely out of place.

Consider the color of path materials. Washed and ornamental stones are often sorted by color, and other materials are available in various colors and hues. Choose a color that you like and that best suits the style and purpose of your path.

Estimating Materials

To order the proper amount of material, you'll have to calculate the number of cubic feet or cubic yards needed. To determine the area in square feet, multiply its length by its width in feet. Then decide on the

MATERIALS

The following materials are available from garden- and landscaping-supply stores, sawmills, quarries, and gravel-pit operations.

SOFT MATERIALS

- Bark mulch (can be sorted by type)
- Wood chips (can be sorted by type)
- Pine needles
- Nut hulls
- Chopped leaves
- Sawdust

HARD MATERIALS

- Pea stone and other washed stone (graded for color and size)
- Crushed stone (graded for color and size)
- Seashells
- Brick chips
- Recycled glass with smoothed edges

appropriate depth of materials and multiply the area figure by that amount. (*Note:* Convert inches to feet by dividing by 12.) Let's say you want to create a path that's 10 feet long, 4 feet wide, and 3 inches deep.

$$\text{length in ft.} \times \text{width in ft.} = \text{area in sq. ft.}$$
$$\text{10 ft.} \times \text{4 ft.} = \text{40 sq. ft.}$$

$$\text{area in sq. ft.} \times \text{depth in ft.} = \text{cu. ft.}$$
$$\text{40 sq. ft.} \times \text{0.25 ft.} = \text{10 cu. ft.}$$

Keep in mind that the finish layer should be thick enough to conceal the base but not so thick that it hinders walking. A too-thick layer of soft materials is an uncomfortable walking surface and apt to find its way into walkers' shoes, whereas a thick layer of washed stone is a challenging walking surface, akin to walking on dry beach sand or ball bearings. Ask your supplier how much you can expect a particular material to compact and order accordingly.

With path area and depth in hand, review the following to estimate how much material you need. These materials are usually purchased in cubic yards; 1 cubic yard of loose-fill material covers 324 square feet, 1 inch deep; 162 square feet, 2 inches deep; 108 square feet, 3 inches deep; 81 square feet, 4 inches deep; and 54 square feet, 6 inches deep. Buy about 10 percent more than you calculate is needed to account for spilling and loss.

Site Preparation

After laying out your path (see page 85), remove any obstacles, such as large rocks, that have not been incorporated into your design. If the path passes through thick underbrush or low-hanging branches, clear the way for the walker by pruning and trimming.

Preparing the Base

Installing a base that drains well will improve the quality and longevity of your path.

Remove sod and other plant materials that you don't want to keep. Then excavate the path to the appropriate depth, removing any rocks or roots as you go, always trying to keep the base level. When you've reached the proper depth, install the base material.

Crushed gravel is the material of choice because it's readily available, compacts tightly, and provides good drainage. To minimize labor, work in sections. If possible, have the gravel delivered near the path, then move it by the wheelbarrowful. This prevents overfilling, something that happens easily if the full load of gravel is dumped in the path itself.

CALCULATING EXCAVATION DEPTH

Base thickness varies somewhat according to soil condition and climate, but 4 to 6 inches is the average; poor-draining sites require a slightly deeper base. Calculate the total excavation depth by adding together the depth of the base you need and the depth of the path material. This sum is how deep you have to excavate if you want the path flush with the surrounding ground. If you want the path elevated slightly from surrounding ground, adjust the base depth or the depth of the path material accordingly.

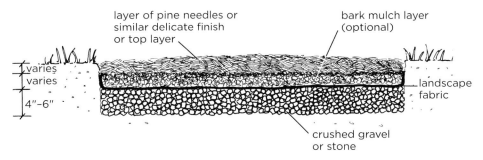

layer of pine needles or similar delicate finish or top layer

bark mulch layer (optional)

landscape fabric

crushed gravel or stone

varies

varies

4"–6"

Installing landscape fabric over a crushed-gravel or stone base prevents fines from the finish and buffer material from infiltrating the base and compromising its ability to drain properly. ▪

After you fill and level a section, moisten it with a garden hose, then compact it. A hand tamper usually works well on a loose-fill path, but a water-filled roller, or for larger jobs a vibrating-plate compactor, can also be used. Compacting decreases the volume of the base material, so you may need to add and compact more gravel to attain the desired base depth. Next, install landscape fabric.

Adding Bark Mulch

If you'll use a delicate soft-fill material such as pine needles or salt-marsh hay for the finish layer, you'll want to add a buffer, or cushioning, layer of finely ground bark mulch. This slows the breakdown of the finish material and creates a comfortable, springy feeling underfoot. As was done for the gravel, spread the bark mulch, water, and tamp.

Installing Finish Material

Installing the finish material is easy. It's most convenient to have it delivered and dumped near the path site. From there, it's just a matter of moving it, load by load, and spreading it to the desired thickness.

Edging

Edgings are essential for hard materials and can help tame potentially unruly soft materials, such as wood chips. Soft materials that bond together, such as bark mulch and pine needles, don't scatter as easily as wood chips and thus are better suited to a borderless look.

If you want to give your loose-fill path a formal look, edging is a must. For example, a loose-fill path that leads to the front door of a house should have a substantial but properly scaled edging that relates to the house and complements the color of the path; the edging should also counter the informality of the loose-fill materials. Bold edgings are most easily used with wide paths because they are similar in scale.

To choose an edging, keep the qualities of the finish material in mind. A continuous, gapless edging works best for hard materials, which tend to slide and shift when walked on. A more decorative edging, such as round beach rocks, may be appropriate for soft materials, which tend to compact and stay in place when walked on. Other types of stone (cut,

A BASELESS PATH

If the soil drains readily, you can create the path without installing a gravel base. Simply lay it out, remove sod if any, then dig to the desired depth — a level 2 to 3 inches works well. Remove any stones or roots, then install landscape fabric. Landscape fabric provides a buffer between the ground and the path material, inhibits weed growth, and keeps the path material from becoming embedded in the soil. Last, install the path material, wet it, and tamp.

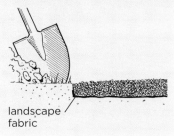

landscape fabric

cobblestone, blasted) or bricks and timbers also work well as edging for loose-fill paths. Plastic edging looks too artificial for my taste.

Edgings that are partially buried in the ground, such as cobblestone and brick, are installed when the base is prepared. Those that rest on top of the ground, such as round stones and timbers, are installed after the finish material is in place. (See page 90 for edging options.)

Maintenance

To look their best, loose-fill paths require maintenance; plan to weed, rake, and replenish the path material as needed.

Even with a gravel base layer and landscape fabric, shallow-rooted weeds sometimes pop up in a loose-fill path. Do your best to keep up with them. Pull weeds before they seed, preferably just after a rain, when the ground is soft and the roots come up easily.

Raking keeps the path looking neat and allows you redistribute the path material if there are any bare spots. If there are large bare spots, add more path material. Keeping extra path material on hand is always a good idea and helps ensure a good match. It is possible to order extra material after the fact, but the color may not be the same and, of course, it will cost extra to have a separate load delivered, no matter its size. If you need extra materials and can't find precisely the same type, order enough new material so you can blend it thoroughly with the old.

The stones used in this formal edging easily hold the loose-fill material in place and also make a beautiful edging for the flower beds.

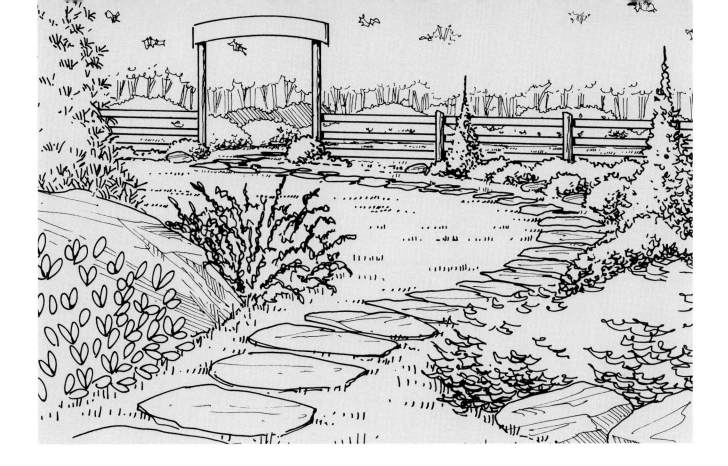

STEPPING-STONE PATHS

Stepping-stone paths have an appealing, nostalgic quality and a rich history. For centuries, stepping-stones have punctuated the spiritual journey to the traditional Japanese teahouse, emphasizing the transition from routine, worldly cares to a place of rest and reflection. Stepping-stones demand our attention and encourage us to focus on the journey, not the destination.

Stepping-stone paths can be made from a broad range of materials: flagstone, masonry pavers, and wood rounds all work well. (For simplicity, in this section *stepping-stone* and *stone* refer to any of the materials recommended for use in stepping-stone paths.) Although these paths are typically considered informal, they can be made to look formal with careful planning. For example, in a manicured flower garden, a neat, predictable path design is appropriate. This can be achieved by choosing like-shaped materials, such as cut stone and rectangular concrete flagging, and surrounding them with ornamental stones and a prominent border.

There are two basic approaches to constructing stepping-stone paths: the stones can be cut into an existing lawn individually or the entire path can be cleared, the base prepared, the stones set in, and the area around the stones filled in or planted. The latter approach is better for rough or unplanted ground.

The following materials can be used in stepping-stone paths and are typically available through garden-, landscaping-, and masonry-supply stores and at sawmills and quarries. You also may be able to gather them yourself.

■ Irregular flagstone

■ Regular or cut flagstone

■ Concrete flagging (precast, or make your own as described on page 58

■ Masonry pavers

■ Wood rounds

Estimating the number of stepping-stones needed is simply a matter of considering the average size of each and the proposed length of the path, then doing simple math.

Appropriate Uses

The spacing of stepping-stones controls a walker's gait, speed, and focus. Stepping-stone paths are especially inviting when they curve or meander through the landscape. Use stepping-stones in gardens when you want to draw the walker's attention to specific plants or objects, from a deck to a garden, as an entrance to a woodland path, even through boggy areas or across a shallow stream if you don't want to build a small footbridge.

Unless the stepping-stones are very large, say 2 feet by 3 feet, these paths are not well suited for utilitarian purposes. When you're carrying packages from the car to the house, the last thing you want is to be concerned about where you put your feet. Stepping-stones also are not the best choice for a path to the front door; guests should feel comfortable and at ease when approaching your house.

DETERMINE CENTER-TO-CENTER SPACING

The first important task when designing a stepping-stone path is determining the most comfortable spacing between the stones. Begin by measuring your average stride and the strides of other adults in your home who will use the path; this gives you a range of possible center-to-center spacings. If the stride lengths are different, a compromise is in order. For example, my natural stride is about 26 inches and my wife's is about 22 inches. When constructing our stepping-stone path, we settled on a 22-inch center-to-center distance and used large stones to help make up for my longer stride.

Once you have determined the center-to-center distance, lay out the path (see page 85), then stretch out a tape measure along one side. Insert a small stake or pin flag where the center of each stone should be located.

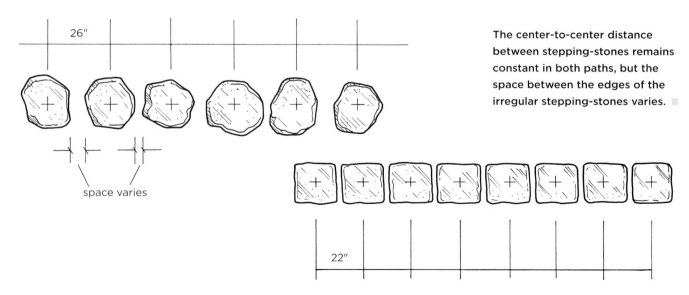

The center-to-center distance between stepping-stones remains constant in both paths, but the space between the edges of the irregular stepping-stones varies.

Preliminary Layout

With the center-to-center distance established, it's time to consider the arrangement of the stepping-stones. During this critical step, you will also determine the size and number of stepping-stones you need.

Laying out stepping-stones is part science, part art. Although the center-to-center distance is fixed and set by stride length, you are free to choose the size, shape, and orientation of the stones. Create cardboard or plywood templates cut to the size and shape of the stones you're considering, then place them on the ground. This helps you visualize what the finished path might look like and gives you an opportunity to try it out before buying any materials.

As you experiment with the templates, step back from time to time to reflect. Will the stepping-stones be large enough or do they look lost in their surroundings? If used in a small space, are they too large?

And what about the spaces between them? Do they look too small or too big? Because the center-to-center distance is fixed, you'll adjust stone-to-stone spacing by choosing larger or smaller stepping-stones.

Keep playing with template size and layout until you are satisfied. That way you can order your materials with confidence, knowing that you're buying the right size and quantity of stones. During installation, you'll probably make some minor adjustments, but using the templates as a guide will simplify your work considerably.

Experiment by incorporating stones of different shapes and sizes in your design. Also, remember that you can control the walker's stride length and cadence by altering stone size and the distance between the stones. ▦

Site Preparation

Whether you cut stones into the ground individually or prepare the entire base, clear the way for the walker by pruning underbrush and branches that intrude on the path and removing any plants, rocks, or roots that are in the way.

Preparing the Base

Before digging, decide how the stepping-stones will relate to the surroundings. I like to set them so they're ½ to ¾ inches above ground. Keeping their profiles low makes maintenance easy. If you set stones into the lawn individually at this height, for example, you can mow right over them. Stones set higher than this don't allow for this convenience and can be a tripping hazard for walkers. (If the area surrounding the stepping-stones is subject to standing water, however, you'd have good reason to set the stones above the water level, but it might be safer to consider a different option, like a boardwalk or footbridge [see page 143].) Stones set flush with or lower than the ground surface might look good on a dry day, but on stormy days they become catch basins for rain; they are also prone to being overgrown and covered by grass and leaves, and thus require more maintenance.

To prepare the entire base for a stepping-stone path, first lay out the path, making the width about 2 to 4 inches wider than the stepping-stones; this extra room makes it easier to set the stones. Next excavate to the proper depth and backfill with gravel, compacting each 3-inch layer as it is added. Remember to take stepping-stone thickness into account when adding gravel.

To cut individual stepping-stones into the ground, the process is pretty much the same. However, in this case, after the path is laid out a base is prepared for each individual stone and the lawn or ground cover surrounding it is preserved.

Installing Stepping-Stones in Lawn

First, lay out stepping-stones along the length of the path, maintaining the proper center-to-center distance. Spaces between regularly shaped stepping-stones are even and consistent, but fitting irregularly shaped stones takes time and an artist's eye — they may have to be trimmed. Walk the path to see how it feels, then stand back to see how it looks. Make needed adjustments now.

TIP

If the soil doesn't drain well or is subject to heaving, prepare a crushed-gravel base to a depth appropriate for local conditions, probably between 6 and 12 inches.

With a square-nosed spade or an edger, make a cut in the lawn about 1 inch larger than the perimeter of the stone. Set the stone aside, remove the sod, excavate to the appropriate depth, then install and compact the base. Nestle the stone into place and tap it with a rubber mallet, making sure it's level side to side. Heavy stones virtually set themselves because of their weight, but lighter stones take a bit more work.

Continue setting stones in this manner, checking your work as you go. Are the stones stable? If not, now is the time to make adjustments. Last, fill in the gaps around the stones with strips of removed sod, or add topsoil and sow seed. (For information on grass types and the best times to sow seed, see page 96.)

Installing Stepping-Stones in a Prepared Base

After the base has been prepared, lay out stepping-stones along the path length, maintaining the proper center-to-center distance. Walk the path to see how it feels, then stand back to see how it looks. Make needed adjustments now.

Set the first stone into the base at the correct height and level it side to side. If the thickness of the stones varies, the depth of the base may need to be adjusted to maintain proper height. Continue working in this manner, double-checking center-to-center distance as you go. Walk the path again to see how it feels. Are all the stones stable and set to your liking? If not, make the appropriate adjustments.

Last, fill the spaces with loose-fill material, moss, or some other type of ground cover. (See Filling the Gaps on page 115.)

Maintenance

Stepping-stone paths require minimal maintenance. If set slightly above the level of a lawn to allow for easy mowing, you may need just to sweep them clean. Stepping-stones are easy to reset if they sink or shift out of level, and are also easily replaced if broken.

SOLID PATHS

Of the paths discussed thus far, solid paths are most obviously the work of human hands. They safeguard walkers from idiosyncrasies of the ground's surface and are made of materials that fit together precisely in simple or intricate patterns. These paths require patience and skill to lay out and install, and are more expensive to create than the other paths in this chapter, but the result is definitely worth the effort. Solid paths are useful in formal settings and high-traffic areas.

The path material and method of installation contribute to the overall look and feel of the path. A herringbone pattern creates an elegant front walkway but may not be suitable for a path to the back door, where a simple running bond might be a better fit. When choosing materials and pattern, consider the impression you want it to make. You'll find a wealth of ideas and possible combinations in home and gardening magazines and at masonry-supply stores. See page 56 for some common patterns, or experiment and create a pattern of your own.

Two types of materials can be used in solid paths: flagstone pavers, such as cut stone, irregular stone, and precast concrete flagstone; or modular pavers, such as brick pavers, masonry pavers, and cobblestone.

Flagstone pavers tend to be large and thin and are typically fit together like puzzle pieces. Modular pavers, on the other hand, are usually small and bricklike, allowing you to create intricate patterns.

Appropriate Uses

Make a solid path for a broad, elegant walk to the front door, a service path from the garage to the side or back door, a utility path to a tool or garden shed, a safe way to get from the patio to the pool, or a narrow path through a well-kept flower garden. The only place where a solid path might not be appropriate is cutting boldly through a natural setting, such as a field or woodland.

Site Preparation

After laying out the path (see page 85), clear the way for the walker by trimming anything that encroaches on the path, like brush or low-hanging branches. Also, address the problem of tree roots if necessary (see the box on page 112).

Base Preparation

Solid paths require extensive base preparation. Base depth is determined by climate and soil conditions. In locations where soils drain well and the ground doesn't freeze, solid paths can be installed on a 3- to 4-inch sand base, but a more substantial base provides a more stable, longer-lasting path.

First, determine the finished height of the path, which may be slightly above the surrounding ground or flush with an existing step or patio. When you excavate, you must account for the desired finished height, the thickness of the pavers, and the depth of the base, typically 6 to 12 inches.

To ensure that the pavers are well supported, the base must be wider than the finished path. Flagstone pavers are supported over a broad area and so require less support than modular pavers. For flagstone pavers, plan to excavate the base 4 to 6 inches wider than the finished path on each side; for modular pavers, excavate the base 6 to 12 inches wider than the finished path on each side.

Remove sod, then excavate the base to the appropriate width and depth. Level and compact the bottom. If the ground drains poorly, install landscape fabric to inhibit soil infiltration and provide added stability.

Next, install the base material. Use crushed gravel as a base for flagstone, and crushed stone as a base for modular pavers or if conditions are poor. (Crushed stone compacts more tightly and is more stable than crushed gravel.)

MATERIALS

You can find these materials at garden-, landscaping-, and masonry-supply stores, and at quarries and salvage yards.

FLAGSTONE PAVERS

- Irregular flagstone
- Regular or cut flagstone
- Fieldstone
- Concrete flagstone

MODULAR PAVERS

- Cobblestone
- Brick pavers
- Masonry pavers

Order solid path materials by the square foot. Your supplier can help you decide how much you need, but the basic process is as follows. First, determine the area of your path by multiplying its length by its width. Next, if you'll use modular pavers, determine how many pavers fit in a square foot, then *multiply* the path area by that number. If you're using regular flagstone pavers, determine how many square feet one paver covers, then *divide* the path area by that number. Irregular flagstone is typically sold by the square foot, not by the piece.

To account for estimating errors, mistakes, and breakage, it's a good practice to buy slightly more material than you think you need.

Tree roots can wreak havoc on a solid path. Nothing is more disheartening than to see a carefully laid path bulge and buckle over time. If you encounter tree roots when preparing the path base and don't want to risk problems later, consider rerouting the path, making a different type of path, or cutting back the tree roots at least 2 feet from the path's finished edge. If the tree is a prize specimen, consult an arborist: cutting the roots can injure or kill the tree.

Proper preparation and execution are critical if you want your solid path to last. When in doubt, be conservative and err on the side of caution. ▓

Spread the base material evenly along the length of the excavation, working in 3-inch layers. Wet and compact it after each 3-inch layer is added.

Last, prepare to lay in a bed of mason's or concrete sand. The setting bed must be level and of consistent thickness; the sand will compress about ⅜ when compacted. Place 1-inch pipes on the base material at the outside edges of the finished path and confirm that the pipes are level across the path's width and length. Secure the pipes in place with U-shaped anchoring pins or by partially burying them with gravel. (If the path will curve, use a pipe bender to bend pipes accordingly.)

Add the sand, then rake it out to fill the path evenly. Rest a 2×4 screed across the pipes, then work it back and forth in a sawing motion along the length of the path to level the sand. Remove the pipes. If you are making a flagstone path, compact the setting bed now.

Installing the Finish Material

Irregular flagstone suggests unique patterns, and assembling such a path is like fitting together the pieces of a puzzle. A creative eye will help you design an appealing path. Cut stone, precast concrete, and masonry pavers are usually installed in regular, predictable patterns.

Spaces between flagging pavers can range from ⅜ inch to 1 inch but should be consistent to maintain the visual continuity of the path. For regular flagstone, the spacing can be gauged by eye or with a tape measure, but a faster method is to use a precut ⅜- to 1-inch spacer as a guide. Pavers are installed with small spaces between them, which are then filled with sand. Smaller spaces make a path look formal, whereas wider spaces make it look relaxed and informal.

Concrete pavers typically have spacer nibs that maintain a ⅛-inch gap; most clay pavers do not have spacing nibs. Spacing between pavers should range from ¹⁄₁₆ inch to ³⁄₁₆ inch: ⅛ is optimal. Brick pavers can be set with wider spacing, but the result will be a less stable path surface.

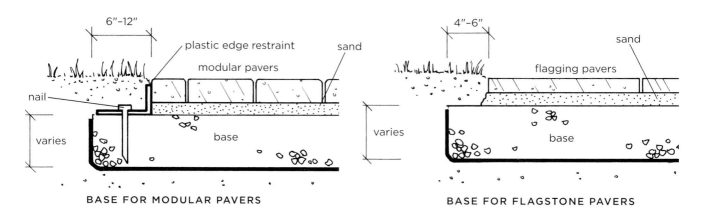

BASE FOR MODULAR PAVERS

BASE FOR FLAGSTONE PAVERS

STARTING THE PATTERN

Before beginning to lay out a pattern, determine the best starting point. For modular paving, it's best to begin the pattern at the most important fixed point. For example, the pattern for a walkway from a front door to a driveway should start at the front door. This way you'll set a full pattern where it is most visible and will address any shortfall in the pattern at the other end.

For regular flagstone, work from the middle out to the ends. You'll compensate for any problems at the ends of the path by cutting material or adjusting the spacing.

For irregular flagstone, work in from the edges toward the middle. First, set stones with long, straight sides along the edges of the path. You'll fit and cut stone as needed as you work in from the edges. (See page 51 for more on cutting and fitting techniques.)

GUIDE STRINGS

Set guide strings to help keep everything straight. Make the string taut and set it about an inch above the pavers. Check your work frequently. On a sloping path, set the string at the proper pitch to ensure that the path runs evenly. (See page 85 for more on using strings for path layout.)

TIP

For easy access and efficiency, have pavers delivered as close to the path site as possible, then distribute them along the length of the path. This is especially helpful when laying out irregular flagstone, because after you place a stone, you'll need to hunt for the next stone that will fit best.

Guide strings help keep path edges straight and true. Check your work frequently.

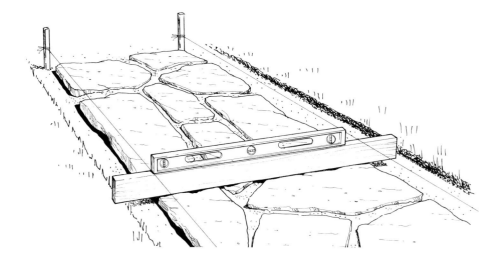

Make sure that each individual stone is level and that the path is level across its width. ▪

INSTALLING FLAGSTONE

Begin a flagstone path by fitting and laying out several feet of path, paying particular attention to spacing, then stand back and see what you think. If you are satisfied, set each piece in the sand by working it back and forth with your hands, then tap it into place with a rubber mallet. As you set each piece of flagstone, make sure it's level; take time now to make any adjustments. Lay a 2×4 across the width of the path and check it for level. Use guide strings to ensure that the path is level or at the proper slope; if it's not, adjust.

Continue working in this fashion, checking your work regularly. Walk the path with a critical eye and make any necessary adjustments. When you are satisfied, install the edging (if you're planning to use it), and finish the job by filling in the gaps (see below).

INSTALLING MODULAR PAVERS

Modular pavers are installed much like flagstone, except for the final bedding procedure. Nestle the paver into the sand and tap it into place with a rubber mallet, being careful to maintain consistent spacing as you work. Lay a 2×4 across the width of the path and check it for level. Guide strings also help you determine whether the path is level or at the proper slope; if not, adjust.

If you plan to incorporate a border, such as a soldier course (see page 56) or a special concrete paver shape, in your paver design, install it as you install the pavers.

Installing Edgings

Although edgings are not required, they enhance the structural integrity of a path of masonry pavers. If you haven't yet chosen an edging style, see page 90 for some ideas.

If you prefer structural support only, use an edge restraint. Edge restraints are typically made of plastic and are designed to provide an "invisible" stable edge for pavers. Install them following the manufacturer's recommendations.

Bedding the Pavers

Use a vibrating plate compactor to make two or three passes in each direction. This will settle the pavers uniformly into the setting bed and level the path surface. Next, fill or plant the gaps.

Filling the Gaps

Filling in the gaps between flagstone and modular pavers has decorative and functional benefits and is an important last step in path construction.

Soft materials, such as bark mulch, wood chips, and pine needles, diminish hard edges, giving a path a casual air. They tend to gray over time and are most easily used with widely spaced pavers.

Hard materials, like ornamental washed stone, crushed stone, and seashells, are available in a variety of colors. Materials that approximate the color of the pavers will blend in; contrasting colors, on the other hand, set off the pavers, accentuating their shapes and patterns.

Before beginning, be sure the spaces are deep enough to hold the material in place — 1 inch is usually enough. Spread the material over the path, then brush it into the spaces with a push broom.

The tight spaces between modular pavers should be filled with mason's sand. After the path has been mechanically compacted, spread dry sand over the path, then use a push broom to force the sand into the spaces.

Planting the Gaps

Planting the gaps softens hard edges, introduces color and contrasting texture, and ties the path to adjacent plantings.

Many different types of plants, such as grasses, moss, and ground covers, can be used, but the best choice will depend on the location of the path, the width of the gap, and your climate. If the path passes through a lush lawn, for example, filling the gaps with grass might be a wise choice.

Enlist the help of a local nursery, garden store, or landscape designer when choosing plants. Then prepare the space by removing sand and gravel to a depth of 2 to 4 inches. Add an appropriate growing medium for the plants you've chosen, then set them in and water well. The first few weeks after planting are critical for any plant, so be vigilant: water and shade or protect them as required until they are well established.

Maintenance

Maintenance chores vary with path type and location. Flagstones or pavers may need resetting, edgings may need to be repaired and replaced, and the fill may need to be topped off. If the path appears to be buckling or heaving, you'll probably want to investigate; tree roots may be encroaching on the path.

Steps

5

STEPS HELP us negotiate changes in elevation in a comfortable and efficient way. Utilitarian and decorative, they can integrate seamlessly into a building's landscape or serve as a bold architectural feature. When judiciously placed, steps can link different areas of your property, making them easier to access.

Use steps, perhaps in conjunction with low retaining walls, to distinguish one area from another, such as the lawn from a garden, or specific zones within a garden from each other. A broad set of on-grade steps adds drama to the approach to your front door. And steps built into a large, gently sloping lawn become a bold focal point.

How will you incorporate steps into your landscape? Is there an obvious need? Do you have a particular location in mind? This chapter helps you assess and evaluate the site you are considering and then walks you through construction of a safe, pleasing set of on-grade steps. We begin with an overview of steps and some guiding principles and then move on to specific projects.

Types of Steps

Given the many configurations of stairs that you've probably climbed in your lifetime, it might be hard to believe that there are only three principal types: straight run, helical, and composite. Straight run and helical steps are unique types, whereas composites are a combination of the two.

Straight-Run Steps

The shape of the treads and the resulting line of travel distinguish straight-run from helical steps. In straight-run steps, the tread depth is consistent from side to side and the line-of-travel is straight ahead. A straight-run stair does not change direction, even if a landing is introduced. Of the three types, straight-run steps are the easiest to lay out and build and the most commonly used outdoors. They provide a direct approach and work well when used in conjunction with paths.

Straight-run steps provide a direct approach. Choose materials appropriate for the setting. If steps will lead to a formal entrance, as in this example, materials should reflect that.

Helical Steps

Helical steps — also known as spiral, circular, or winding stairs — feature pie-shaped winder treads. In a helical step, the outside edge of the tread is wider than the inside edge. When several complete revolutions are installed, the steps form a helix shape. The line of travel in helical steps is an unbroken curve that moves around a center point and maintains the same arc from beginning to end. Full-revolution helical stairs are beyond the scope of this book, but incorporating a few winder treads in your step design allows you to change direction gracefully and to gently guide someone around a point of interest or obstacle.

This step design incorporates a straight-run section, a landing, and a helical component. The curve adds interest and intrigue as the steps wend their way to the next level of the garden.

Composite Steps

Composite steps combine elements of straight-run and helical steps to introduce a change of direction. The simplest type of composite step incorporates a straight-run, a landing, and a straight-run with a different orientation from the first. Virtually any combination can be used: successive sections of straight-run and helical steps, sections of straight-run and helical steps linked with landings, and helical sections that curve in opposite directions are just three possibilities. This versatility makes composite steps useful in landscapes and gardens, where steps must be adapted to fit unalterable, sometimes awkward conditions.

Design Considerations

Steps are paths that take a slightly different form. Accordingly, they serve many of the same functions that paths do and are influenced by similar factors. (For an overview of issues to think about, see pages 73–85.)

The Psychology of Steps

Steps profoundly impact the way we move. Understanding how we experience steps is a critical component of good stair design. As you begin to think about steps, ask yourself what effect you want them to have.

Studies show that people are more comfortable ascending steps than descending them and that descending steps is more dangerous. That may be because on the ascent, we face the steps and can reach out to catch ourselves if we slip. Conversely, on the descent, we face away from the steps and have farther to fall, which tends to make us proceed more carefully.

Because our eyes are closer to the level of the stairs when we ascend steps than when we descend them, we are in a better position to see

Terms to Know

Before we consider step design in detail, it's important to understand four essential concepts: rise, run, riser, and tread. Rise and run are units of measure, whereas riser and tread are components of a set of steps.

Rise is a vertical distance. *Total rise* is the distance from the bottom to the top of the steps and the *unit rise* is the height of an individual step. A *riser* is the physical object (a board, for example) that spans the rise. An *on-grade riser* is usually a solid piece of wood or a stone or stones. A *return* is that part of an on-grade step that is perpendicular to the riser and forms the side of the tread.

Run is a measure of horizontal distance, or length. The *total run* is the overall length of the entire set of steps and the *unit run* is the length of one step. *Treads* are the members that span the run of an individual step.

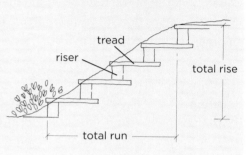

STEPS OR RAMP?

Steps connect areas that are at different elevations. They use space efficiently, spanning a given height in a much shorter distance than is possible with a ramp, and are meant for foot traffic, not wheeled traffic. Before adding steps to your landscape, be certain that they will facilitate rather than impede movement. Whether steps or a ramp is most appropriate depends on the intended use and principal users.

what's directly in front of us. Placing low flowering plants or similar items at the edges of steps adds visual interest, slows down walkers, and may make climbing steps more enjoyable.

On long stairways, landings offer welcome respite. If the landing is large enough, place a bench or chair there to encourage walkers to sit and relax. To motivate walkers to continue on their upward trek, at the head of the stairs consider placing a tall goal that can be seen only partially from the landing, such as a plant or statue, as a visual reward. But be aware that what holds our attention when we climb stairs will probably be ignored as we descend. When walking down steps, particularly if they are unfamiliar to us, our natural tendency is to focus on our feet.

When descending steps, landings help to arrest forward momentum, particularly if the flight of steps is long. For interior steps, building code dictates the frequency of landings, but for exterior steps, let the requirements of the site, common sense, and walker safety help you decide what's best. Landings provide ideal opportunities for taking in expansive views and vistas if you have them to share.

Step design is necessarily influenced by site conditions, but the choices you make also profoundly affect how the steps are perceived and experienced. For example, the approach to a front door can be made simple and direct with a straight run of steps or elegant and dramatic with a set of steps that arc gently. A straight run of steps hastens a journey, whereas steps with turns and curves slow it down. Turns and landings in steps that meander through a hillside garden echo the landscape and encourage the walker to pause and enjoy.

Secondary Uses

Steps make excellent pedestals for displaying plants, statuary, and found objects. Emphasize the natural rhythm of steps by placing objects in a series, perhaps decreasing or increasing in size as the stairs ascend, or punctuate the beginning of the steps with large, low planters.

Steps are often used as impromptu seating and can be a great spot to enjoy a distant view or sunset or to talk casually. People tend to gravitate to the top or bottom of steps when sitting, so make the steps a comfortable size to encourage this.

Site Assessment and Planning

You'll want to choose a step style that relates to the surroundings, including buildings, lawn, gardens, and any paths they will connect with. What is the predominant style? Is it formal or casual, modern or traditional, simple or complex, or some combination? Does your house date to a particular period or have a distinct architectural style? If yes, how might you address this in your steps? You may want to choose a complementary style for one area and a contrasting style for another.

Before you begin dreaming of the ideal set of steps, consider potential locations and do some preliminary on-site investigation. Walk through the property, imagining different possible layouts. Next look at the reference points on your preliminary site plan and mark overlays with the approximate spots where the steps might be located (see chapter 2 for more on preparing a site plan). Keep notes on what you learn, such as:

- *What will you see at the top and bottom of the steps? Have you considered these views?*
- *Will the sun strike a portion of the steps or all steps, creating a warm, inviting place to sit?*
- *Even though one route is the most direct, would a small shift one way or another enhance a view or move the steps into, or out of, the sun?*
- *If you live in a warm climate, can you situate the steps in such a way to take advantage of overhanging trees?*
- *Are there spots on the stairway where you might want to pause or change direction?*

Consider other possible stair layouts, then on overlays draw steps that best suit your particular site and goals.

When faced with a design challenge, look for opportunities. On Block Island in Rhode Island, grassy paths cut through old fields of preservation land bounded by stone walls. Instead of breaching the walls, which would have needlessly destroyed a piece of history, the path designers built A-shaped steps that go up and over the walls, preserving them for future generations.

Determining Step Dimensions

Step dimensions greatly impact the look and feel of steps. By experimenting with the overall width of a flight of steps, the depth of the individual treads, and the height of the risers, you can create steps with different personalities. Broad stairs with short risers and deep treads present a stately appearance, whereas stairs with high risers and short treads are more businesslike. Wide, clearly visible steps are welcoming, whereas narrow ones, perhaps partially concealed with plants or grasses, are mysterious. A set of steps that begins wide and ends narrow beckons us forward and focuses our eyes on the destination. Looking down from the top, these steps seem to open up to the surroundings, inviting us to explore.

Although steps may vary in width, the height and depth of individual steps must remain fairly consistent and predictable for reasons of safety. Any significant riser and tread changes should occur only in conjunction with a landing.

Types of On-Grade Steps

On-grade steps are constructed directly on the ground. This connection with the earth gives them a solid, secure feel and allows for the use of a variety of building materials and rise/run configurations.

The simplest type of on-grade steps is made with stepping-stones. A series of "stepping-stones," which can be stone, concrete, or even wood rounds, are cut into a hillside. The result is rustic and informal and will work well in a natural-looking garden or on a wooded hillside. (As in chapter 4, in this section *stepping-stone* and *stone* refer to any of the materials recommended for use in stepping-stone stairs.)

Walking on stepping-stones requires careful attention. The width of the step is determined by the size of the stone, and the structural integrity of the step is determined by the stability of the soil; no base is needed.

Stair widths and possible uses

WIDTH	DESCRIPTION/USE
1'–2'	Very narrow steps; perhaps stepping-stone steps on an open slope
2'-6"–3'	Standard-width steps; good size for use in a garden or short elevation
3'-6"–4'-6"	Generous steps; work well for steps to front door
5'–6'	Broad steps; make a strong statement at a front door and are likely to encourage sitting. Two people can walk side by side
6' or more	Very broad; stairs this wide are real eye-catchers and look best if they have relatively low risers

Frequent maintenance is essential to keep these steps passable. If located in a grassy area and not attended to regularly, the steps will be quickly overgrown. (See page 105 for a discussion of stepping-stone paths.)

Steps with earthen treads are usually constructed from logs, timbers, or boards set on edge. The risers are dug into a hillside, and the treads are the ground. The treads may slope from riser to riser, depending on the pitch of the ground. For them to remain stable, the risers must be secured in the ground with stakes or long metal spikes driven in at their front edge or through them.

Steps with infill treads are more substantial. In these steps, timbers or logs are typically used for risers, but stone curbing is also an option. Any of the materials used in paths can be used for these treads, but some choices are better than others. Brick and concrete pavers, precast concrete, and small pieces of flagstone are excellent tread options. Grass, on the other hand, is slippery when wet, and pea stone will migrate onto solid risers, making the walking surface potentially treacherous. To construct these steps, excavate the area for the first two steps, set a riser in place, and partially backfill the tread portion. Continue working in this way for all steps. Last, install the tread material.

The most substantial and longest-lasting steps covered in this chapter are one-piece steps and drystone, or mortarless, steps. In one-piece steps, one thick slab of stone comprises the riser and tread. Drystone steps are the most labor-intensive and complicated on-grade steps to build. Multiple stones are used for the risers and one or more stones for the treads.

Materials

Select step materials after you settle on a step type and style. Choose materials that are long-lasting and appropriate for the look and feel you hope to achieve. Rot-resistant materials are durable and always good choices. Highly finished materials, such as cut stone, lend a formal air to steps. Hand-shaped stone and rough-sawn or unfinished wood tend to be casual, whereas fieldstone and wood timbers are rustic and unassuming. Striking results can sometimes be achieved by using a combination of rough and finished materials. When possible, choose native materials over nonnative materials. These will probably look at home in your setting, no matter the design of the steps.

Spend time exploring your neighborhood and town, looking for inspiring and interesting ways to put materials together. (For more on materials, see chapter 3.)

TIP

Stone is heavy. Because of size limitations and the weight of stone slabs, you may need to place two or more pieces side by side to achieve the desired tread width.

WHY NO CONCRETE?

As explained in chapter 3, use of concrete requires some degree of expertise and efficiency, and formal applications are best left to professionals. In addition, concrete is rigid, tends to crack over time, and is difficult to repair. For these reasons, concrete steps and materials that require concrete foundations are not discussed in this chapter.

RISERS AND RETURNS

■ **Wood:** Logs and timbers of rot-resistant species; timbers and boards of rot-resistant species or pressure-treated with a preservative.

■ **Composites:** Landscaping timbers of composite materials.

■ **Stone:** Almost any stone appropriate for paths.

TREADS

■ **Wood:** Rot-resistant or pressure-treated timbers for solid treads; bark mulch or wood chips.

■ **Stone:** Stone slabs, irregular or cut flagstone, washed stone, crushed stone.

■ **Masonry:** Brick pavers, concrete pavers, precast concrete, skid-resistant tile.

■ **Plants:** Grass and hardy ground covers.

Put It on Paper

Once you've decided on a type and style of step, sketch some possible designs on overlays to your site plan. Experiment with several options before settling on one design. (See chapter 2 for more on preparing a site plan.)

Planning Considerations

Once you've completed the aesthetic aspects of step design, tackle the technical tasks and see how your vision works in a real-world application. To be properly and safely designed, steps must be kept within a relatively narrow set of parameters; the rise needs to be consistent and predictable. Unlike indoor steps in which a difference of more than $\frac{3}{16}$ inch is unacceptable, some on-grade steps are not built to such close tolerances. We tend to expect the unexpected in the outdoors, which is a great help because even well-built on-grade steps may settle over time.

Total Rise and Total Run

Step design is based on rise and run, with *rise* being the vertical measure and *run* the horizontal measure. To refine your design, you need to know the total rise and total run for the planned steps.

The *total rise* is the vertical distance that a flight of steps travels. For example, a slope that drops 3 feet has a total rise of 3 feet. Easy, right? The concept of total run is a little trickier.

Total run is the horizontal distance traveled by a flight of steps. While total rise is a given dimension, total run is determined by the design of the stairs and can be adjusted to fit a specific situation. For example, if the slope mentioned above is 6 feet long, measured horizontally from the top to the toe, the total run is 6 feet. A set of steps could be designed to conform to that total run, or it could be designed to have a different run altogether.

Rise and Run

To create the steps, divide the total rise and total run into equal, appropriately sized units. Rise and run dimensions should comfortably accommodate the human gait. I find that a unit rise between 5½ and 7 inches is most comfortable and practical for outdoor use. The minimum run for on-grade steps is 12 inches.

In properly designed steps, the run decreases as the rise increases. When building outdoor steps, where space is usually at much less of a premium than it is indoors, you have more run options because the

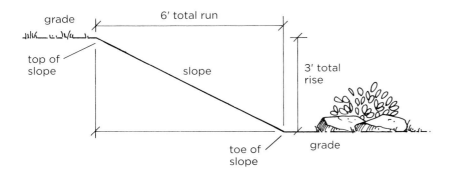

grade

top of slope

slope

6' total run

3' total rise

toe of slope

grade

◀ The total rise and total run of a slope are measurable dimensions, but the total run of the steps is determined by their design and can vary from the total run of the slope.

ground can support treads of greater depth. You might choose between a standard, one-stride step and a deeper, two-stride step, for example.

ONE-STRIDE STEP Standard on-grade steps require a 12-inch minimum run. Because a shorter rise should be matched with a longer run, it's better to pair a 6-inch riser with a 15- to 18-inch unit run; likewise, a 7-inch riser is best with a 12- to 15-inch unit run. While it's possible to have even longer treads, at some point deep treads become awkward for walkers. Treads longer than 18 inches would probably cause someone either to lengthen her stride or cut her stride short. If you want deep treads, design a two-stride step.

TWO-STRIDE STEPS Two-stride steps are deep enough to allow you to take two steps on the same tread. To maintain a regular stride, pair a 6- to 7-inch rise with a 20- to 36-inch unit run. Here again, 6-inch risers are more effectively paired with 24- to 36-inch-deep treads and 7-inch risers with 20- to 24-inch-deep treads. Treads deeper than 36 inches are more properly considered landings and would be awkward to walk on, perhaps resulting in just less than three strides. Try out different rise/run combinations to determine what's most comfortable for you.

▶ One-stride steps are safer and more comfortable when built to these parameters. Note that the return defines the width of the step and supports the riser above it.

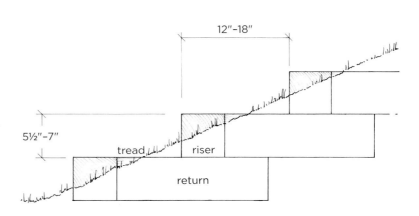

12"–18"

5½"–7"

tread

riser

return

Cheeks

The most straightforward on-grade steps closely follow the pitch of a gentle slope. As earth is dug to make room for the steps, the resulting sides of the steps form *cheeks*. The deeper you dig into the slope, the bigger the cheeks. Earthen cheeks can either be allowed to slump into the top of the treads or be held back by *cheek walls* made of timbers or stone. If the cheek walls will be a foot or two higher than the treads, incorporating a stone or timber retaining wall is a good idea; construct it *before* the steps. (To learn more about constructing stone retaining walls, see Charles McRaven, *Stonework*. North Adams, Mass.: Storey, 1997.)

Landings

Landings are intended to slow forward momentum and can be thought of as extra-large stair treads. For landings to do their job properly, they must be obvious. On interior steps, building codes regulate landing size. Typically, indoor landings are the same width as the steps and at least as long as the steps are wide; a 3-foot-wide stair would require a 3-foot-long landing, for example. Outdoors, landings built to this minimum dimension will probably seem too small. Whenever possible, be generous with landing lengths and expand them to 4 feet or more if space allows.

Finalize the Design

You now have all the information you need to refine and complete the design of your steps. Once you've created the layout, selected the materials, and determined where the steps will be located, it's time to calculate the length and height of the steps. I'll walk you through an example. When doing your own calculations, simply insert the relevant data for your project. The calculations will help you determine the appropriate rise/run combinations for the steps.

Designed to closely follow the slope of the hill, *A* shows the first riser at the toe of the slope. To accommodate a certain tread length and to achieve the proper riser-to-tread relationship, occasionally steps must be set into the hill *(B)*; in *B*, the first riser is set in from the toe of the slope one tread length.

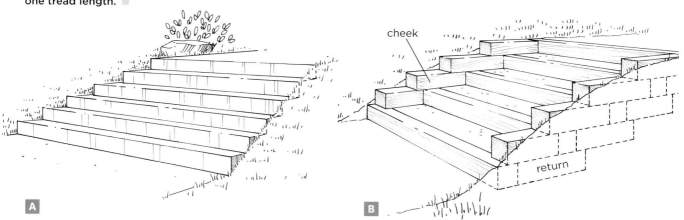

A

B
cheek
return

To make it easier to visualize this process and to avoid mistakes, draw a large-scale profile and plan (½" = 1') for the proposed steps.

Let's assume that from the top to the toe of a slope, there's a total rise of 3 feet and a total run of 6 feet. Assuming that we'd like easy, low-rise steps to climb, we'll begin the calculation by trying a 6-inch unit rise.

$$36\text{-inch total rise} \div 6\text{-inch unit rise} = 6 \text{ risers}$$
$$6 \text{ risers} - 1 \text{ tread} = 5 \text{ treads}$$

This yields a total of six risers and, therefore, five treads for this set of steps (in a flight of steps, there is always one less tread than riser).

To determine the run, divide the total run by the number of treads:

$$72\text{-inch total run} \div 5 \text{ treads} = 14.4 \text{ unit run},$$
$$\text{or approximately } 14\tfrac{3}{8} \text{ inches}$$

A 6-inch rise paired with a 14⅜-inch tread is acceptable, but a longer tread would be a better match (see chart on page 128). Be aware, however, that increasing the run to 18 inches would require increasing the total run from 6 feet to 7 feet 6 inches (18 inches × 5 treads = 90 inches, or 7 feet 6 inches), which means the steps would have to be cut farther into the hill, possibly requiring cheek walls, and the location of the top step altered or pushed out farther at the bottom, thus exposing the tread returns and shifting the location of the bottom step.

If steps begin at the toe of a slope *(A)*, some treads have exposed returns and others have cheeks. If steps are set into the toe of the slope one tread length *(B)*, a cheek wall is required at the top of the steps. Even though the total run of the steps in *C* and *D* are identical, notice the impact of the difference in the slope's run for each: 72" versus 48"; *D* requires a substantial cheek wall.

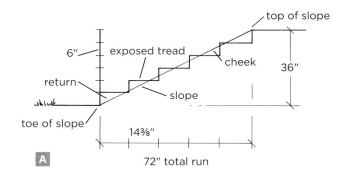

A

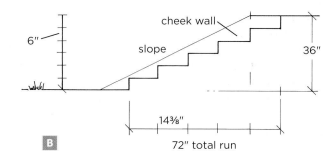

B

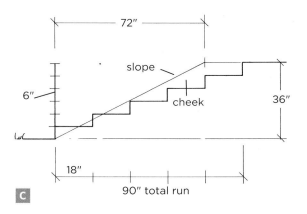

C

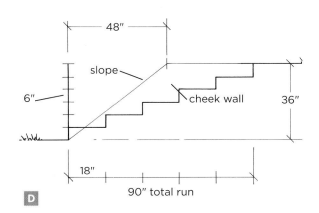

D

Rise/run in on-grade steps*

STAIR TYPE	SUGGESTED UNIT RISE (STEP HEIGHT)	SUGGESTED UNIT RUN (TREAD)
One-stride	5½"–6½"	15"–18"
One-stride	6½"–7"	12"–15"
Two-stride	5½"–6½"	24"–36"
Two-stride	6½"–7"	20"–24"

*These are guidelines only.

Estimating Materials

Use the scale drawings of your steps to estimate the materials you need. Have someone at the local building-supply store double-check your work for you before you make any purchases. You will need to estimate the quantities of:

- *solid or loose tread material.*
- *riser and return material, if it's separate from the tread.*
- *material to hold back cheek walls, if necessary.*
- *gravel, sand, or suitable base and bedding material; see page 58.*

Building Your Steps

On-grade steps are built, quite literally, from the bottom up: the bottom step is constructed first and successive steps are more or less stacked on top of it. We will be looking at five types of on-grade steps: stepping-stone steps, steps with earthen treads, steps with infill treads, one-piece steps, and drystone steps.

Prepare the Ground

The first task is to mark off the location of your steps. Roughly locate the steps on the ground by referring to the reference points on your site plan. Then stake an area about 2 to 3 feet wider and longer than the steps you plan to construct. You'll need to account for the width of the steps as well as for any retaining walls that will be built.

Probe the ground with an iron bar for obstacles such as rocks and ledge. If you find anything, dig around it with a shovel to see whether it can be removed easily. If the obstacle seems large, you'll want to relocate the steps to avoid it, incorporate it into the design of the steps, or consult an excavator.

Roots can also cause problems. As they grow, they can cause steps to heave and buckle, so plan to remove any roots that seem to threaten the steps. Consult with an arborist or professional landscaper to be certain that removing roots won't compromise a favorite plant or tree.

If you're making steps with earthen treads, steps with infill treads, or drystone steps, cut and peel away any grass or sod in the marked-out area. Also remove and save any topsoil. When you've finished clearing the ground, remove the stakes. Skip these steps if you're making stepping-stone or one-piece steps.

Lay Out the Steps

With the ground cleared, finalize the location of the steps and verify the total rise. Starting at the bottom of the steps, stake the location of the first riser and the overall width of the steps.

Next, establish the location of the top of the steps. If you are building straight-run steps, plumb up from the location of the first riser, measure out the total run (the distance from the first riser to the last riser), and stake the location of the last riser; see illustration on page 132.

To verify that the steps are "square," measure the diagonals from the first riser to the last riser, then adjust the top stakes until both diagonals are of equal length. If the steps will incorporate winder treads, see the box on pages 130 and 131.

If the hillside that you are building the steps into has a cross slope and slopes from side to side as well as from top to bottom, the ground on one side of the stairs will be higher than the other. Therefore, the riser might be flush with the ground on one side and a cheek may be needed to hold back the ground on the other side.

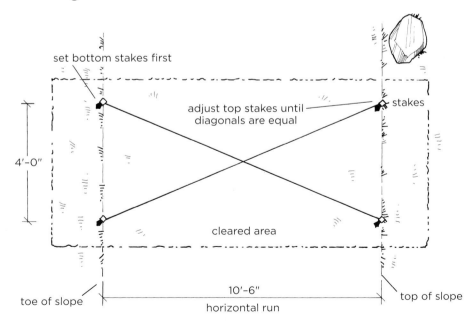

set bottom stakes first

adjust top stakes until diagonals are equal

stakes

4'-0"

cleared area

toe of slope

10'-6"

horizontal run

top of slope

After clearing the area around the steps, stake the location and width of the first riser. Next, measure the length of the steps and stake the location of the last (or top) riser. Square the steps by measuring the diagonals along the slope and making needed adjustments. Keep the tape measure taut to ensure accurate measurements.

Laying Out Steps with Curves and Winders

Laying out curved steps is more complicated than laying out straight-run steps. In this example, we add a curve at the top of straight-run steps, but the same technique can be used in most other situations.

1. Locate the toe of the slope, then stake the location of the first riser and the total stair width. Next, lay out the run to the last riser of the straight-run portion. Leave space for the curved portion of the steps, then stake where you want the steps to end at the top.

Lay out the curve between the top of the straight-run portion of the steps and the top of the steps. Use two hoses to approximate the curve on your plan as closely as possible on the ground. Experiment with the inner and outer arcs until you get them right; they should be parallel. Secure the hoses in place with metal or plastic hose hoops.

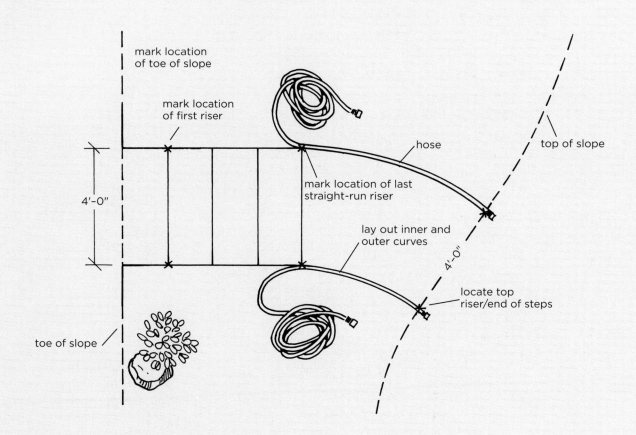

mark location of toe of slope

mark location of first riser

hose

top of slope

4'-0"

mark location of last straight-run riser

lay out inner and outer curves

4'-0"

locate top riser/end of steps

toe of slope

2. To determine how wide to make the pie-shaped winder treads, first measure the overall length of each curve. These measurements need to be taken on a level plane, so depending on the length of the curve and the grade of the slope, you may need help with this. For shorter distances, simply bend a tape measure so it follows the curve. For longer distances, drive grade stakes at appropriate intervals to follow the curve, then mark level lines on the stakes from the top of the slope and measure the distance. If the curved section of the slope is extremely long — for example, the entire length of the slope — you will have to mark the stakes with level lines that are lower than the initial marks.

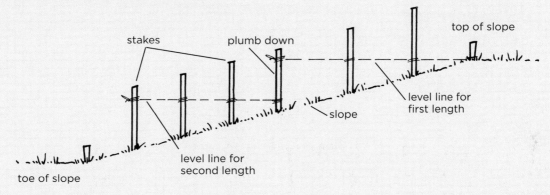

3. When you have determined the lengths of the curves, divide each by the number of treads to arrive at the outside and inside tread lengths. Stake the tread locations on the ground.

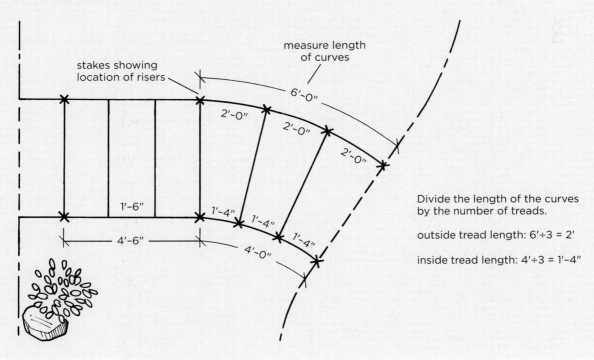

Divide the length of the curves by the number of treads.

outside tread length: 6'÷3 = 2'

inside tread length: 4'÷3 = 1'-4"

Measure total run of the steps with the aid of a level, then measure total rise. ▦

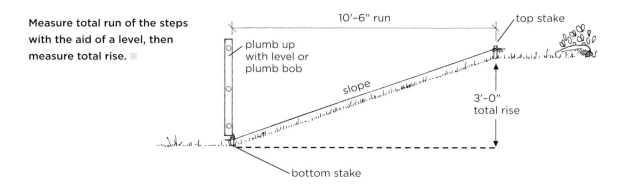

10'-6" run
top stake
plumb up
with level or
plumb bob
slope
3'-0"
total rise
bottom stake

Adding a landing to steps decreases the total rise, and therefore riser height, for a given run of steps. Account for this during layout. ▦

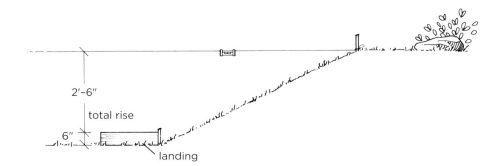

2'-6"
total rise
6"
landing

Once the bottom and top of the steps are staked, measure the total run of the steps using a level or plumb bob. Then measure the total rise. If you will include a landing, the total rise is measured from the top of the landing to the top of the slope. With these heights set, put a level on a straightedge or pull a line level from the top of the steps to measure the vertical distance (the total rise) and compare it to the dimension you used during the design process; site preparation may have altered it. If the total rise is significantly different, a discrepancy of 2 to 3 inches for example, you may need to adjust the riser heights, or in the case of one-piece risers, the total rise.

Install offset stakes 2 to 3 feet outside the excavation area to define the top and bottom of the steps and the width of the steps. When building the steps, run guide strings between the stakes to locate the position of the first step; refer to guide strings to keep steps running true.

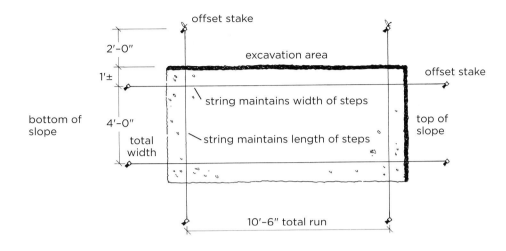

offset stake

2'-0"

1'±

excavation area

offset stake

string maintains width of steps

bottom of slope

4'-0"

total width

string maintains length of steps

top of slope

10'-6" total run

Use the top and bottom stakes to set offset stakes. When offset stakes are in place, remove top and bottom stakes so they aren't in the way during construction.

Install the Base

Steps need a solid base that provides adequate support. If you live in a mild area and have stable soil that drains well, bare ground might be the only base you need; simply remove any topsoil or surface organic materials and build the steps. If the soil drains poorly and is subject to freezing, a substantial base is especially important.

The base is meant to provide a buffer from the effects of the seasonal freeze/thaw and swell/shrink cycles. Create a proper base for steps with a layer of crushed, compacted gravel, the depth of which is determined by local soil conditions. Well-draining, stable soils might require only 6 to 12 inches of gravel, whereas wet, clay-type soils might need a 12- to 18-inch layer. (See page 89 for more information on base construction.) Crushed gravel makes an excellent base because it is easy to install, compacts uniformly, and drains well.

Base Preparation

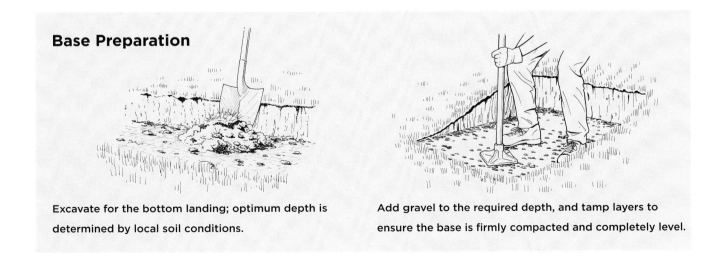

Excavate for the bottom landing; optimum depth is determined by local soil conditions.

Add gravel to the required depth, and tamp layers to ensure the base is firmly compacted and completely level.

Start constructing the base for on-grade steps at the bottom. If there will be a bottom landing, excavate for it and the first step, then fill it to the proper depth with gravel. Even if there won't be a landing, you might want to excavate, backfill with gravel, and regrade the area with topsoil so it drains quickly after a rain. After the landing and first step are constructed (see box on page 133), then excavate and backfill the next section of base. Continue working this way until you reach the top of the steps.

If you choose to use timber or stone risers, allow their returns to extend at least 6 inches beyond the back edge of the next riser; this will provide support for the riser and stability for the return of the step above it. In this example, shown from above *(A)* and the side *(B)*, a 2-foot return supports the next riser return.

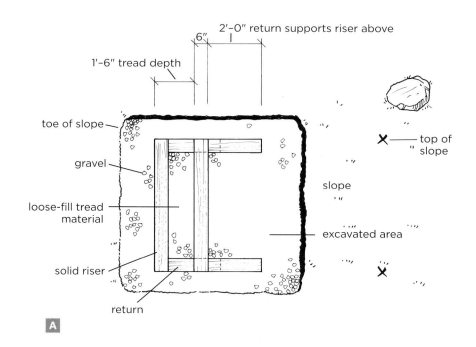

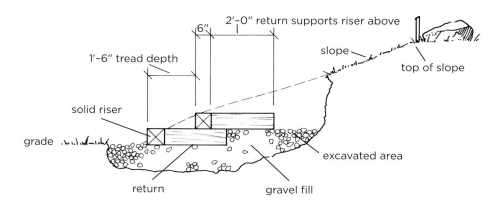

STEPPING-STONE STEPS

Stepping-stone steps follow the pitch of a slope precisely and thus are laid out by eye and set into the existing grade. Soils that drain well may require no special base. The stones should be large and heavy so they won't move or dislodge when stepped on. In soils that drain poorly, crushed gravel can be used as a base to increase stability.

Start work at the bottom of the slope, making a level cut to accommodate the stone. Nestle the stone in place, allow for planned riser height, and repeat. Space stones so they are a comfortable distance apart. Hillside vegetation stabilizes the ground between stepping-stones, so disturb the riser area as little as possible when installing the stones. Replant any damaged areas, and if necessary use stone supports until vegetation grows back. Make each riser equivalent to the unit rise, less the thickness of the tread. If a slope is particularly steep, you may need to incorporate stone riser supports.

Angling stepping-stones slightly forward can eliminate the need for riser supports. However, be aware that if steps pitch forward too much, they won't provide adequate footing, especially when wet.

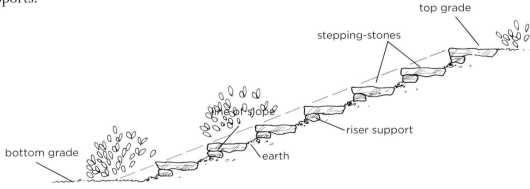

STEPS WITH EARTHEN TREADS

Like stepping-stone steps, steps with earthen treads follow the existing grade and can be built without a prepared base. Landscaping timbers, logs, and thick boards make good risers. The process is simple: lay out the steps and calculate rise and run (do not prepare a base), install the bottom riser, level the tread area, allow for proper riser height, and install the next riser.

Begin by installing the bottom riser. Secure timbers and logs in place by driving 2-foot lengths of #4 (½-inch) rebar through predrilled holes. If you use thick boards, bury the bottom edges and secure by driving a metal stake at the front edges of the boards on the left and right.

Next, level the tread area. Depending on the slope, the hill may spill into the tread area; the steeper the hill, the more tread area the slope will cover. Steep slopes will require more steps, so their treads may be small.

Secure timbers or logs in place with rebar *(A)* or by burying and staking *(B)*. ▦

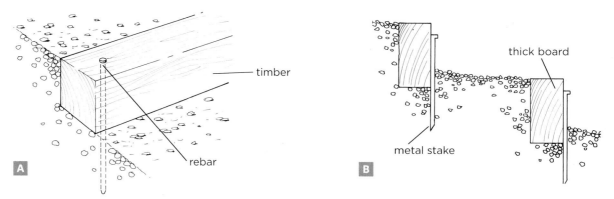

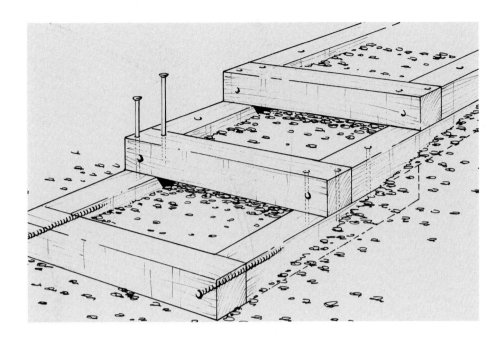

STEPS WITH INFILL TREADS

These steps are built from one-piece wood or stone risers and tread material such as masonry pavers, washed stone, bark mulch, or grass. Prepare the base as described on page 133. Ground can be allowed to slump onto the stairs, or wood or stone cheek walls can be installed for a more finished look.

When the first section of the base is compacted to the desired depth and is level, set the first riser in position, using the stakes marking the front edge of the first step as a guide. Next, cut the returns (see illustration on page 134) to the proper length and set them in place. Make sure that all is level, and use a framing square to ensure that returns are perpendicular to the riser.

If you are using timber risers, secure them to the returns with large timber screws; timber screws are more effective than spikes. It's good construction practice to predrill pilot holes and countersink the screws. Alternatively, use a half-lap joint (see page 68) to attach risers to returns.

Double-check to be sure the returns are square, then backfill the tread area with gravel and compact. Allow enough room at the top to accommodate the depth of the finish tread material. Plan to use 1½ to 2½ inches of loose-fill material.

Prepare grass treads and masonry pavers as described for grass paths on page 95 and for solid paths on page 111.

Continue working in this manner until the steps are complete.

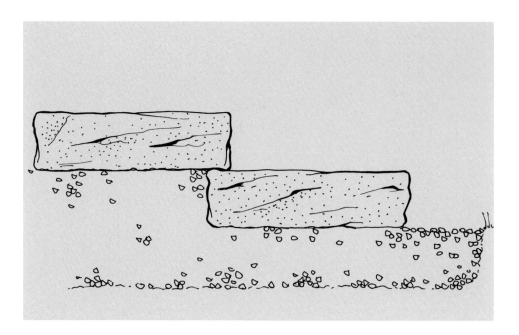

ONE-PIECE STEPS

One-piece steps are constructed with materials that are thick and deep enough to function simultaneously as riser and tread; stone or masonry is typically used. The stones required for one-piece steps, generally from 5 to 6 inches thick and 14 to 18 inches deep, are heavy and difficult to maneuver, but installation is straightforward. When purchasing materials, be sure to allow for a 2- to 3-inch overlap between steps. Prepare the base as described on page 133.

Before installing each step, double-check to be sure the base has been prepared to the proper depth and is level from side to side and from front to back. Depending on its size, the step can be moved into place with a hand truck or rollers and a pry bar or some other lever. Position the first step and check it for level. If necessary, lift up the stone and remove or add base material.

With the first step properly set, excavate for the second step, filling and compacting the base until it is level and flush with the top of the first step. Allow a 2- to 3-inch overlap between steps for stability.

DRYSTONE STEPS

Drystone steps are constructed without mortar. These steps are typically composed of multiple-piece, built-up risers that are capped with one-piece or multiple-piece treads. Stone and masonry are usually the materials of choice.

Prepare the base as described on page 133. Beginning on a level, compacted base, construct the first riser to the proper height (riser height minus tread thickness). In addition to the riser, construct returns to both support the tread on the sides and minimize the chance that the treads will settle. If the treads will consist of more than one piece, construct a hidden riser at the back of the tread for more support. Then backfill and compact behind, and to the level of, the riser.

Remember that the tread must be deep enough to support the next riser. With the first tread in place, excavate, backfill, compact, and level, then build the next riser and place the tread. Continue working in this manner until the steps are complete.

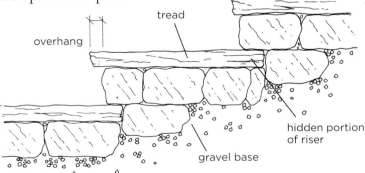

Drystone steps can be constructed with the tread overhanging the riser slightly. Treads must be of sufficient length to support the riser above. ∎

Footbridges 6

B UILT TO A HUMAN SCALE, footbridges complement the landscape. They can be used decoratively to visually link two distinct areas or to signal a transition. Of course, they also have a practical application and can span divides such as gullies, ditches, and streams.

This chapter is about planning and building four kinds of residential-scale footbridges: plank, boardwalk, joisted, and simple-truss. None spans a long distance, and all can be used for a broad range of applications. They do not require complicated engineering and are built with readily available materials and basic tools; construction techniques are similar to those used in building decks. Follow the plans presented here precisely, or modify them to suit your needs and preferences.

Types of Bridges

A bridge is categorized by how structural forces act on and through it. There are four types: beam, cantilever, suspension, and arch. In beam bridges, the forces push down at the ends of the bridge, whereas in a cantilever bridge the forces push down and up at the ends of the bridge. Suspension bridges pull, and arch bridges push, against the ends of the bridge. The footbridges in this chapter are based on the beam-type bridge.

Beam bridges are by far the simplest. A familiar example is a log across a stream. When someone stands in the middle of a log bridge, his weight is distributed equally to each bank through the log. The forces in a multispan beam bridge are a little more complicated but are basically the same, with each support carrying its share of the load.

The forces developed in a beam bridge are compression and tension. *Compression* is crushing force, and a material's resistance to it is called *compressive strength*. *Tension* is a force that pulls a material apart; resistance to it is called *tensile strength*.

For a beam material to be effective, it must possess both compressive and tensile strength; wood does, and that's why logs, timbers, and planks have been used successfully for beam bridges of all sizes. Stone, on the other hand, while it has more compressive strength than wood, is very weak in tension. When used for beams, stone spans are short and structural cross sections large when compared to wood. However, the superior compressive strength and overall durability of stone makes it an excellent choice for bridge supports, which are under compression when weight is applied to a bridge.

To overcome the limitations of the available building materials, bridge builders searched for ways to extend the spanning capacity of beam bridges. Projections that jut out underneath a bridge to provide additional support, called *corbels*, and brackets were used.

But it was not until the relatively late development of the truss that significant increases in spans and load were achieved. The truss redistributes a portion of the load from the center of the bridge to the supports. The strength of trusses derives from how compression and tension are distributed.

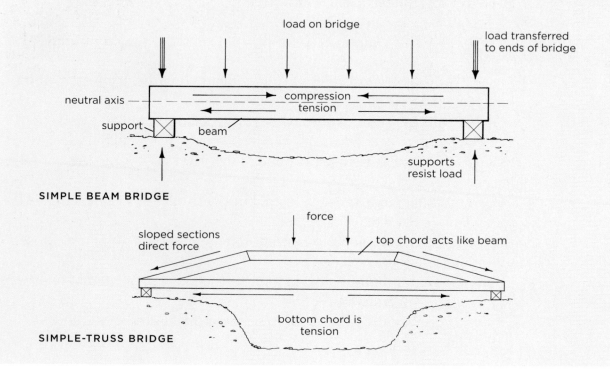

load on bridge

load transferred to ends of bridge

neutral axis

compression

tension

support

beam

supports resist load

SIMPLE BEAM BRIDGE

force

sloped sections direct force

top chord acts like beam

bottom chord is tension

SIMPLE-TRUSS BRIDGE

Which Type of Footbridge?

Once you've decided that you need a footbridge, you have to determine which type you'll build. Although the footbridges in this chapter can be used in various situations, some are better suited to certain applications.

Plank footbridges are picturesque, particularly when spanning shallow water or wet, boggy areas. Their simplicity is part of their appeal, but they are not suited for everyday use or utilitarian functions. Before you decide to build a plank footbridge, do a little on-site investigation to determine whether it's feasible.

Boardwalks are elevated, wooden paths. Although boardwalks can be constructed over shallow water or sandy areas, we will focus on applications you might encounter near your home. Boardwalks can be particularly useful in areas that are uneven or frequently muddy, such as a path to the front door, backyard, or toolshed. They can also be used in a flower or vegetable garden to make walking or pushing a wheelbarrow easier.

Joisted footbridges are similar to boardwalks but with two significant differences. While boardwalks hug the ground, joisted footbridges are typically used to span small gullies or streams. In addition, joisted footbridges often incorporate railings. Depending on how high above the ground a footbridge is, the railing may be purely decorative or designed with both safety and style in mind. Use a joisted footbridge in a garden or backyard to complete a path that has encountered an obstacle, to cross a real or imaginary stream, or to serve as the centerpiece of a flower garden.

Truss footbridges take advantage of the load-shifting abilities of the truss and can span longer distances using smaller structural members; however, this may not be the only reason you would chose to build a simple-truss footbridge. It also has a unique and appealing profile. As the arched footbridges common in Asian gardens attest, there is something special about the journey across such a bridge. The sloped sections of the simple-truss footbridge beckon the walker forward, and the level center is a natural place to stop, think, and take in the surroundings.

PLANK FOOTBRIDGE

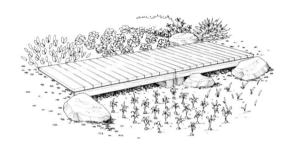

BOARDWALK

JOISTED FOOTBRIDGE

TRUSS FOOTBRIDGE

Building Codes and Wetlands Conservation

The role of conservation commissions is not specifically to prevent work within areas of their jurisdiction — wetlands, streams, and protected riverfront areas — but, rather, to ensure that any work that is performed has no, or minimal, detrimental effects on the protected areas. If your footbridge will span a waterway or wetland, check in with the local conservation commission before you begin construction.

Generally, residential footbridges are considered landscape features, are not regulated by national building codes, and don't require a building permit. However, local jurisdictions often have their own regulations, so it's always best to check with your local building inspector before beginning any project.

Footbridge Components

All beam-type footbridges are composed of four principal components: supports, frame, decking, and railings.

Supports

Supports physically hold a footbridge in place. There are two kinds: abutments and piers. Abutments carry the loads applied to the ends of a footbridge, whereas piers support the footbridge at points in between.

Garden-scale joisted and simple-truss footbridges are single-span footbridges that transmit loads to their ends. The weight of these footbridges — including the *dead load* (footbridge materials) and the *live load* (people walking across them) — is relatively light and predictable. Accordingly, these footbridges are supported by the same type of simple abutments, usually 6×6 pressure-treated landscaping timbers on a gravel base. Simple abutments also are used for the boardwalk design in this chapter.

Plank footbridges are supported by piers. The piers for the plank footbridge design in this chapter consist of two vertical pilings (wood posts) and a horizontal crosstie that connects the pilings and carries the planks. Piers are subjected to *torque*, or side-to-side force, as well as to compression. Torque can potentially "wiggle" and loosen the piers, so the posts must be driven at least 2 feet into the ground (or to frost line depth) to resist this destabilizing force. If you can't install posts properly, don't attempt to build a plank bridge.

Frames

Frames span from support to support and carry the decking. The frame can consist of a single or multiple structural members and must be strong enough to carry dead and live loads.

The planks in a plank footbridge do double-duty as both frame and decking surface. Typically installed flat, boards used this way are much weaker than if they are installed on edge; therefore, the individual planks in a plank footbridge span shorter distances than the boards in the other footbridges we'll discuss.

In boardwalks and joisted footbridges, the frame is 2× dimension stock installed on edge. Its construction is similar to floor framing for a deck. The size and number of joists required depend on the strength of the joist material, length of the span, and on-center spacing of the joists.

The frame of a simple-truss footbridge is made up of individual trusses installed parallel to each other. Each truss is composed of a bottom chord and a top chord. The bottom chord is a single piece of dimension stock that spans the length of the footbridge. The top chord consists of three pieces: one level and two sloping. The four pieces are fastened together securely to form a rigid truss.

Decking

Decking is installed over the frame and is the working surface of the footbridge. If you plan to roll a heavy wheelbarrow across the footbridge, consider using thick, 2-inch to 4-inch pressure-treated planks or rough-sawn lumber from a mill rather than the thinner ¾ stock commonly used to surface decks.

As a general rule, nominal 1-inch- and ¾-inch-thick wood decking can span joists that are installed 16 inches on center, whereas 2-inch decking can span 24 inches on center.

Railings

Railings can be simple and straightforward, highly decorative, or designed primarily with safety in mind. They typically consist of posts, top rails, balusters, and intermediate and bottom rails, or some combination of these.

Posts are the sturdy vertical members that are fastened to the footbridge frame and support the handrails. A railing gets much of its strength from well-secured posts.

Posts can be square, rectangular, round, or turned. Their tops might be flat, beveled, or decorative, capped with a ball or other shape.

> **TIP**
>
> The spanning ability of wood decking is affected by its thickness, species, and grade. Always check with your supplier to verify the spanning ability of the material you plan to use. Do the same for composite materials, which typically have less spanning ability than solid woods of the same dimension.

A post-to-post top rail *(top)* compared to an over-the-post top rail *(bottom).* The latter has a sleeker profile. ▨

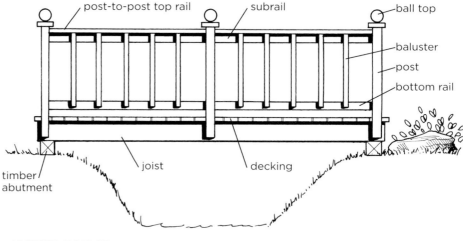

post-to-post top rail · subrail · ball top · baluster · post · bottom rail

timber abutment · joist · decking

JOISTED BRIDGE

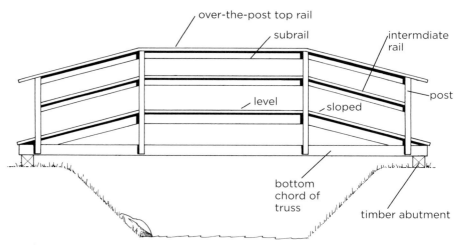

over-the-post top rail · subrail · intermdiate rail · level · sloped · post · bottom chord of truss · timber abutment

SIMPLE-TRUSS BRIDGE

Top rails are horizontal members at the top of the railing system. They are installed on top of, or in between, the posts and may be square, rectangular, or round. The profile of the top rail dictates, to a certain extent, how it will be used. For example, a top rail with a narrow edge or rounded profile is easy to grasp and makes a good handrail. If you want to encourage folks to spend time on the footbridge, lean on the railing, and perhaps set down a drink, choose a top rail that is broad and flat. Handrails can also be flexible and made from rope, cables, or chains; however, this type of railing provides minimal safety and is generally used only decoratively.

Balusters are vertical members that are smaller than posts. They are attached to the top rail and, at the bottom, to either a bottom rail or the footbridge frame. As with posts, balusters may be square, rectangular, round, or turned. The type of baluster you choose and the spacing at which it is installed will dramatically affect the look of the railing system. Baluster spacing also impacts footbridge safety.

If not attached to the footbridge frame, balusters are fastened to a *bottom rail*. Typically made from rectangular stock, bottom rails for footbridges should be designed to shed water, not trap it. The bottom rails for the footbridge designs in this chapter are set on edge.

Horizontal railing systems don't use balusters but instead consist of top, bottom, and one or more intermediate rails. The number of intermediate rails you choose is largely a matter of taste and should be balanced by safety concerns.

Creating Your Own Design

If you want to create your own design by modifying a plan in this chapter, read through the relevant bridge and construction discussions, then build your footbridge on paper. You'll need to create an overhead view (also called a *plan view*) and a side view (also called an *elevation view*). For more on drawing, see chapter 2, Planning.

Make all key decisions first — specifically, where the footbridge will be located, how wide and how high above the ground the footbridge will be, plank thickness, length, and layout — then draw the footbridge to scale. Choose a scale that will allow the bridge to fit on a standard-sized piece of paper. You may want to use ¼-inch scale, instead of ½-inch scale, to fit the drawings on 8½×11-inch paper. You may even find it easier to work on paper that is 8½×14 inches or larger.

As you draw, use tissue-trace overlays to experiment with different design possibilities. For example, after drawing one layout, put a piece of tracing paper over it and draw another. You can do this as many times as you like and compare the different drawings to see which you like best.

If you are uncomfortable using drafting tools, draw your footbridge on graph paper. Nonreproducible, tracing graph paper is a good choice for overlays. Choose a graph paper that has four squares per inch (which is equal to a ¼-inch scale). Designating two

squares for every foot will create a ½-inch scale drawing. Use an architect's scale to mark off inches, and triangles to draw straight, parallel lines. Drawings on graph paper are perfectly suitable for most situations.

Use a non-photo-blue pencil for the scale drawing. Lines made with these pencils won't reproduce when copied, so you can draw lines longer than necessary. After all the elements take shape, trace over the lines with a graphite pencil. Alternatively, draw lightly with a graphite pencil, then darken the lines when the drawing is finished. Always make the finished drawing on tracing vellum or graph, tracing, or bond paper, as these are the most durable.

Once you have your plans in hand, compile a list of needed materials, purchase them, and begin construction. Construction techniques will be similar to those used in this chapter.

TIP: You will want to refer to the plan drawings during construction. Make several copies and keep them on hand in case one gets wet, torn, or ruined.

THE PLANK FOOTBRIDGE

Plank bridges were probably first used in Asian rice paddies. They are ideal anywhere the ground is wet, muddy, or prone to flooding. Because they are constructed in short sections, they can easily be designed to change direction in response to the landscape. Before attempting to build a plank footbridge, do some on-site investigation to see if it's feasible: stable, secure pilings are critical to this design.

If you want to modify the plan provided, first determine the board length and thickness, bridge width, and plank layout; otherwise, after reading the introductory material, turn to page 152. For help sketching your ideas and making a plan, see Creating Your Own Design on page 147.

Board Length and Thickness

My plank footbridge design is built with 8-foot planks. The distance between the piers is 6 inches less than the length of the planks, so the planks will overhang the piers by 3 inches at either end. For an 8-foot plank, therefore, piers are spaced 7 feet 6 inches apart. To safely support the maximum anticipated load — two heavy people standing in the middle of a plank — a nominal 4-inch-thick plank is needed (see chart page 151).

Bridge Width

Another important aspect of plank footbridges is their width. My plank footbridge design is low — 1 foot above the surface of shallow water, boggy areas, or the ground — but, even so, the bridge shouldn't be so narrow that it deters all but the bravest souls from using it. A width of 20 inches feels adequate for most people. Judge for yourself what seems comfortable.

Plank Layout

There are many layout possibilities for a plank footbridge. You can make it go straight, zigzag, meander, or reverse direction. If you made a site plan, you can try various plank layouts by using tissue tracing paper and drawing over it. Otherwise, draw layouts that you think will work for the site you have chosen. For best results, experiment with a few different layouts before selecting one.

The Plans

In my plank footbridge design, the bridge is straight, three planks long, and 1 foot above swampy ground. Each plank is 8 feet long, 3½ inches thick, and 5½ inches wide. The footbridge is 23 feet long (accounting for the 6-inch overlaps) and four planks wide with ½ inch between each board and ¼ inch on either side of the bridge for a total width of 24 inches.

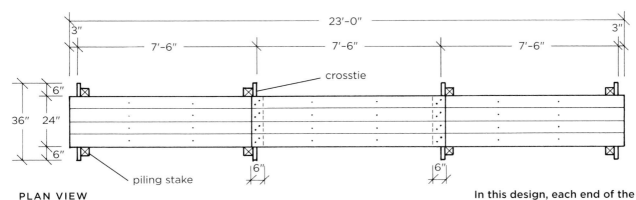

PLAN VIEW

In this design, each end of the center section overlaps the adjacent section by 6″, shortening the overall length from 24′ to 23′. ■

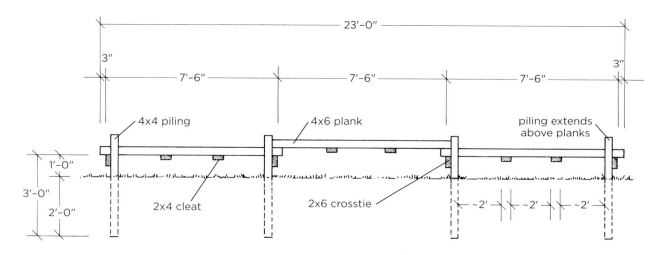

ELEVATION, SIDE VIEW

Note that in the end view *(right)*, the distance between the pilings is 2'-0", or 24", just wide enough to accommodate the four planks, which are 5½" wide, and the three ½" spaces between them. ▪

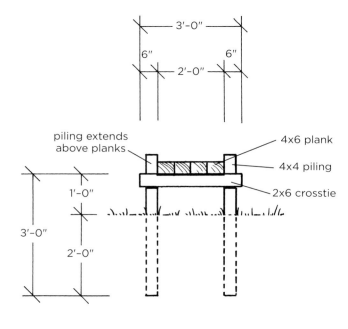

ELEVATION, END VIEW

Note that the piers for my design are made of two parts: 2×6 cross-ties and 4×4 piling stakes. The piers support the bottom planks and are placed in 3 inches from each end of the planks. (The piers are 7 feet 6 inches apart in this design.)

Use the chart on the next page to determine minimum piling length to buy; you'll cut off the extra foot after installation. If you live where soil freezes, make sure the piling extends below the average frost line.

Plank sizes*

Spacing between piers	5'-6"	7'-6"
Plank length	6'-0"	8'-0"
Plant thickness (nominal)	2"	4"

*Pressure-treated southern yellow pine or Douglas fir.

Piling sizes*

SIZE	ABOVE GRADE	BELOW GRADE	FINISH LENGTH	NEED TO BUY
3×3	1'	2'	3'+	5'
3×3	1'-6"	2'-6"	4'+	6'
3×3	2'	3'	5'+	7'
3×3	2'-6"	3'-6"	6'+	8'
3×3	3'	4'	7'+	9'
4×4	1'	2'	3'+	5'
4×4	1'-6"	2'-6"	4'+	6'
4×4	2'	3'	5'+	7'
4×4	2'-6"	3'-6"	6'+	8'
4×4	3'	4'	7'+	9'

*Pressure-treated southern yellow pine or Douglas fir.

Crosstie sizes*

PLANK BRIDGE WIDTH	CROSSTIE NOMINAL SIZE	FASTENERS
12"–18"	2×4	two ⅜"×6" carriage bolts
20"–36"	2×6	two ⅜"×6" carriage bolts

*Pressure-treated southern yellow pine or Douglas fir.

CONSTRUCTING A PLANK FOOTBRIDGE

Now you're ready to order materials and build your footbridge. You can compile your own list of materials, but the list provided is a good starting point. Read carefully through the construction sequence so you fully understand it.

Note: If you choose *not* to use pressure-treated wood, go with a rot-resistant wood of comparable strength, and treat it with preservative as recommended in the text.

Materials

⅔ cubic yard crushed stone for pier base

8 4"x4"x4' piling stakes, pressure-treated for ground contact (longer as necessary to reach below the frost line)

8 2"x6"x36" crossties, pressure-treated

6 2"x4"x24" cleats, pressure-treated

12 4"x6"x8' planks, pressure-treated

Plywood scraps to cover post ends (if driving them into soil)

12 ⅜"x6" stainless-steel or galvanized carriage bolts, washers, and nuts, with which to attach crossties

60 5" #8 stainless-steel, ceramic-coated, or galvanized decking screws, to attach planks to crossties

8 wooden stakes

Marking pen and masking tape

Marking paint or lime

Wood preservative and applicator to treat cut ends

Tools

Bit driver for decking screws

Drill

⅛"x2½" drill bit for predrilling decking

Framing square

Hand tamper

Handsaw

Line level, carpenter's level, or transit

Mason's string

Plane (optional)

Post-hole digger (if needed for digging in dry soil)

Sledgehammer (if needed for driving stakes into wet soil)

Wood clamps

Lay Out the Footbridge

Install a temporary stake (stake 1) at one end of the footbridge, measure out the length of the footbridge (23 feet in this design), and install another stake (stake 2). Drive stakes deep into the ground so they hold securely. Draw a string taut between stakes 1 and 2.

Next, from stake 1, measure out the width of the footbridge (2 feet in this design) and install a third stake (stake 3). To ensure this stake is perpendicular to the line of the first two stakes, pull a string from stake 1 to stake 3 and check the angle with a square; adjust as necessary.

Pull a tape measure 2 feet from stake 2 and another 23 feet from stake 3; install a fourth stake where the tape measures intersect (stake 4). To be certain the stakes are square, measure the diagonals. If the diagonals are equal, the stakes are square; if not, adjust the stakes until they are. (See Keeping Things Square on page 36.)

These stakes outline the perimeter of the footbridge. They will be in your way when it's time to dig holes for the pilings, so install four offset stakes at least 2 feet beyond each corner stake.

ESTABLISH PLANK HEIGHT

Mark the desired height of the crosstie (1 foot in this design) on one of the stakes. Use a level or line level to transfer that mark to the other stakes, then draw the strings taut lengthwise between the offset stakes. These guide strings will help keep the footbridge straight and provide a framework for installation of the pilings.

The layout should be as accurate as possible, but precise tolerances are difficult to achieve when pounding stakes into the ground. Make small adjustments by nudging a stake and packing dirt around its base to hold it in place.

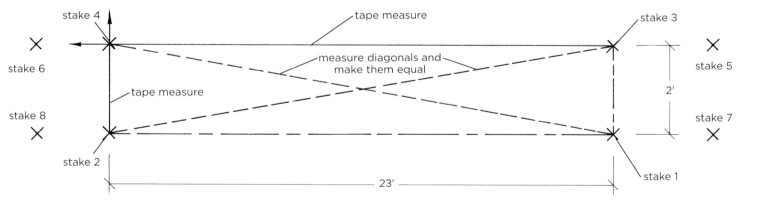

ESTABLISH PIER LOCATIONS

Start by locating the inside face of the first crosstie by measuring in 4½ inches from stake 1. (This accounts for the 1½-inch crosstie thickness and the 3-inch overhang.) Mark this point on the string with a permanent marker, and then place masking tape on the side of the mark where the piling will be located. Repeat this process at stakes 2–4, then mark the locations of the other crossties. One crosstie is used for each pair of pilings.

DECIDE ON BEST METHOD OF PILING INSTALLATION

The most difficult part of building a plank footbridge is installing the pilings, so find out what you're dealing with, then choose the best method of installation for the conditions.

If the ground is just wet or boggy, you should be able to dig a hole for the pilings, either by hand with a post-hole digger or with the help of a power auger. This approach may not work if the pilings need to be installed under water, however (see box on next page).

Drive a metal rod into the ground where the pilings are located to see if you hit ledge or other obstacles. If you don't encounter obstructions, dig some test holes with the post-hole digger. If the hole retains its shape as it's dug, dig holes for the pilings. If the soil is so wet that the holes fill in as you dig them, the most practical alternative will be to drive the posts into the ground with a heavy sledgehammer.

To test this option, sharpen the end of a 3×3 or 4×4 post and try pounding it into the ground. As you drive in the post, notice whether it twists. If it goes far enough into the ground (see the chart on page 151) without twisting, this method should work.

Install the Pilings

Place a temporary stake where each piling will be located, then remove the guide strings. The best method is to remove a string from one stake, coil it, and hang it on the stake at the opposite end.

Dig each hole 2 feet deep (or deeper to reach below the frost line) and reposition the guide strings.

Using the tape marks as a guide, position the pilings outside the guide strings. Slide a piling into the prepared hole on the tape side of the mark, then backfill with crushed stone. Firmly compact the stone every 2 to 4 inches to ensure solid support for the piling. Use a level to ensure the piling is plumb and level. At this point, the piling will be longer than the desired finished height; you'll trim it after the planks are installed.

Installing Pilings under Water

To drive pilings into the ground under water, leave guide strings in place. Sharpen the bottom of a piling, then tack a piece of scrap plywood on top of the piling to protect the wood.

Using the tape marks as a guide, position the piling, then drive it into place. You'll need a helper for this: one person holds the piling; the other drives it with a sledgehammer. Use a level as you work and ensure that the piling is plumb and level. Repeat this process for each piling.

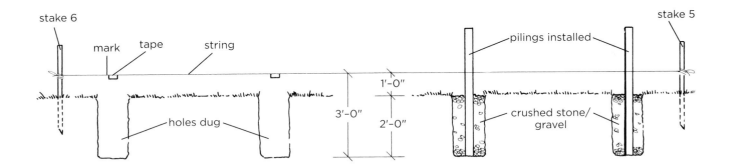

Guide strings assist layout. Here, they're used to locate and install pilings. ▪

Install the Crossties

Confirm that the guide strings are level. Then use them to transfer crosstie height to the installed pilings. Alternatively, use a line level, transit, or a level clamped to a board to mark the top of the crosstie on each piling.

Next, cut the crossties to length (36 inches in this design). Clamp them in place, predrill them, then bolt them securely in position. (See the chart on page 151 for sizes of crossties and bolts.)

Lay Out the Planks

This plank bridge design has three sections. Lay out the first section of planks, top-side down, on level ground, allowing a ½-inch gap between each board. Use a framing square to ensure that the ends are even, then measure diagonally to confirm that the assembly is square. Every third of the way between the pilings (about every 2 feet in this design), attach the planks together with a 2×4 cleat.

When planks that are side by side are walked on, they should deflect simultaneously. That's why footbridges two or more planks wide require boards called *cleats* to tie the planks together. In this design, two 2x4 cleats are screwed into the plank bottoms at regular intervals.

Before fastening the plank sections together, double-check the distance between the pilings. If it is less than 24″, too narrow for a 23½″ assembly to fit, adjust the spacing between the boards accordingly. ▦

When the cleats are in place, flip the first section over (you may need help with this), set it in place, and repeat the process for the last section of the bridge. Confirm that the boards overhang the pilings by 3 inches at each end, then secure them to the crossties with two or three decking screws per plank. Predrill the 3½-inch planks for the 5-inch #8 screws.

Install the middle section of planks last, following the same procedure. The middle section will overlap the first and last section by 6 inches at each end. Predrill pilot holes and secure with screws.

Final Steps

Measure and mark the desired final piling height and cut pilings to length with a handsaw. Use a small plane to make chamfered edges if you want, and treat exposed wood with a preservative.

Finishing Touches

Sand and smooth rough edges and surfaces. Pay particular attention to places that might be prone to splintering. If necessary, glue them with a waterproof glue or nail them in place before they cause problems or get worse.

Apply a sealer or stain to help protect the bridge from the elements. Choose an environmentally friendly, water-based product. You will have to reapply any type of preservative regularly, perhaps yearly, so choose one that is easy to work with.

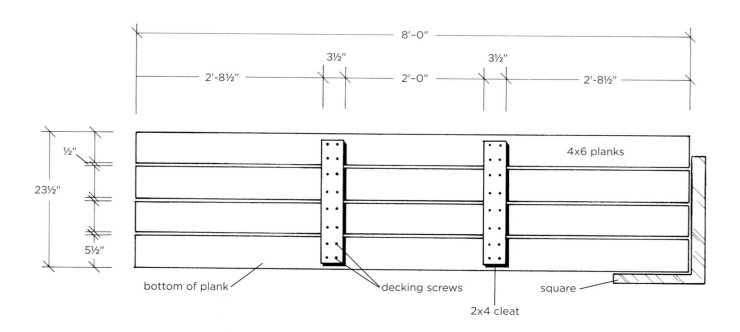

THE BOARDWALK

A boardwalk is essentially a wooden path. It can be straight and direct or it can meander, curve, or zigzag; it can be elevated or low to the ground. My boardwalk design is a straight span built close to the ground. Boardwalks are not well suited for steep slopes; there, paths and steps are better options (see chapters 4 and 5, respectively).

If you want to modify the plan provided, first determine the width and layout. Also consider which decking pattern is most appropriate: perpendicular, parallel, diagonal, or some combination of these. For help sketching out your ideas and making a plan, see Creating Your Own Design on page 147. Otherwise, after reading the introductory material, turn to page 162.

Width

Make the boardwalk wide enough for its anticipated use, but be careful to keep it in scale with the location. Will the boardwalk lead to the front door, from one section of deck to another, or over rough or soggy terrain? Will it be used every day or just once in a while? Will you push a wheelbarrow across it? Use the information in the chart on page 158 to

Boardwalk width and use

WIDTH	HOW MANY PEOPLE FIT?	USE
2' to 2'-6"	One	Minimum width; for occasional or casual use
2'-6" to 3'-6"	One	Easier to navigate
3'-6" to 4'-6"	Two	Minimum for couple; adequate for pushing wheelbarrow
4'-6" to 5' and wider	Two side by side	Easy for strolling hand in hand; minimum entry-path width

help you select the width that is most suitable for your needs. Before settling on a particular width, mock it up to see how it feels.

Layout

If you prepared a site plan, experiment with various layouts on tracing-paper overlays to see what you think. Otherwise, draw layouts that seem suitable for the site you've chosen; try several before settling on one.

As you work on the design, be aware that a boardwalk doesn't have to remain at a constant width. It can narrow or widen as you wish. Vary the width to add interest or to avoid an obstacle. Also keep in mind that boardwalks are best built in short sections.

Decking Pattern

The decking pattern plays a significant role in the look and feel of the boardwalk. Decking installed perpendicular to length accentuates width; decking installed lengthwise accentuates length; and diagonal decking adds visual interest and a sense of movement. The typical arrangement — boards laid out perpendicular to length — works well in a walkway

These are just a few of the possible decking patterns; choose the one you like best. ▓

ALTERNATING DIAGONAL

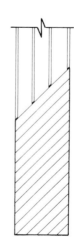

DIAGONAL

blocking

PARALLEL TO JOISTS

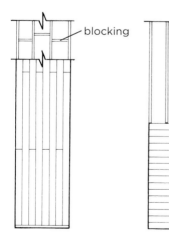

PERPENDICULAR TO JOISTS

leading to a front door, a deck-to-deck connection, or a simple boardwalk through a field. Alternating patterns is also a possibility.

The width of the decking boards will affect the look of a boardwalk. I prefer narrower, 4-inch- to 6-inch-wide decking boards: they're less likely than wider boards to shrink, cup, and split. I also find the smaller scale more pleasing, but wider boards do have their place.

Allowing the decking to extend beyond the boardwalk frame by ½ inch to 1 inch creates an appealing shadow line. Decking also can be installed flush with the boardwalk edge and trim added.

The Plans

Now you're ready to create a framing and decking plan and elevation drawing.

THE FRAMING PLAN The framing plan will be used when ordering materials and to guide construction.

My boardwalk design is 20 feet long, 4 feet wide, and consists of two 10-foot sections. Framing is 2×8 pressure-treated wood, and the decking is installed flush with the frame and then trim added. If, instead, you want the boards to overhang the frame, reduce the width of the frame by the total amount of the overhang. For a 1-inch overhang on each side, for example, the frame width would be reduced by 2 inches, from 4 feet

Draw the perimeter first *(A)*, then add joists and blocking *(B)*.

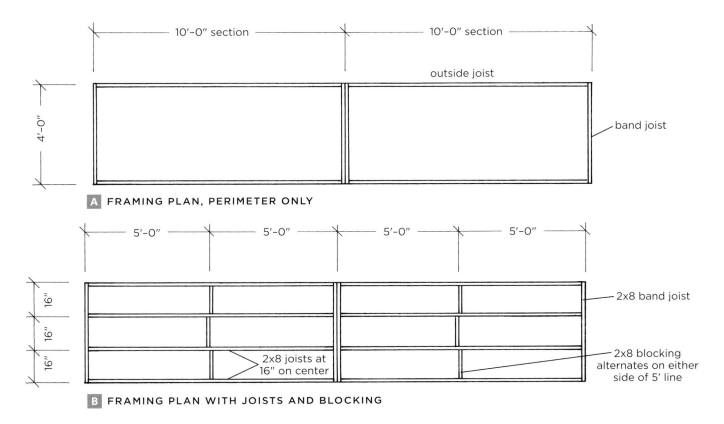

A FRAMING PLAN, PERIMETER ONLY

B FRAMING PLAN WITH JOISTS AND BLOCKING

Boardwalk framing

SECTION LENGTH	ON-CENTER SPACING	SIZE OF JOISTS*
6'	16"–24"	2×6
8'	16"–24"	2×6
10'	16"–24"	2×8
12'	16"	2×8

Note: Use this chart to determine the size and spacing of the joists needed for the boardwalk.
*Pressure-treated southern yellow pine or Douglas fir.

to 3 feet 10 inches. By doing this, the decking can still be 4 feet long, which allows for efficient use of a standard 8-foot board.

Draw the outside joists and band joists for each boardwalk section. The band joists are short boards installed at the ends of the boardwalk sections. Show the thickness of the joists (1½ inches in my design).

Indicate the appropriate on-center joist spacing. (*On-center joint spacing* refers to the distance between the centers of adjacent joists.) The spacing you choose will be a function of the boardwalk span (see chart) and the thickness and spanning capabilities of the decking you choose (see page 145).

Next draw in the blocking. Plan on one row of blocking at the midpoint of joists longer than 8 feet and up to 12 feet.

THE DECKING PLAN Tape a piece of tracing paper on top of the framing plan and draw over it. Make a series of marks along one side of the frame to designate the width of the decking boards. (Decking boards are

In the decking plan, use lines to indicate the decking boards and the spaces between them. ▥

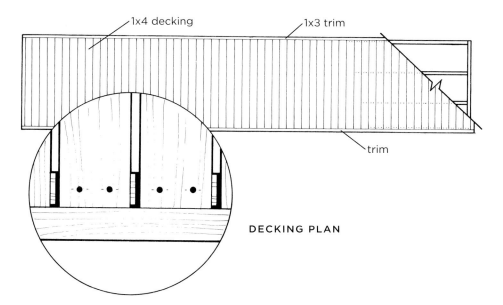

DECKING PLAN

installed with spaces between them, but the spaces are too small to be represented at the scale of the drawing; let the lines represent the spaces instead.) If the decking doesn't end with a full-width board, don't worry about it now. We'll address this issue when the boards are installed.

THE ELEVATION DRAWING Refer to the framing plan and create a side view of the boardwalk to show how it relates to the ground and the position of the supports. Begin by drawing a line representing the ground. Next, draw a line that represents the bottom of the joists, about 2 inches to 3 inches above the ground line. Boardwalks are often installed close to the ground, but because the ground is rarely smooth or level, show the bottom of the boardwalk raised slightly above it.

Next, from the bottom joist line, measure up the thickness of the joists and draw that line. If you don't yet know the decking thickness (see page 145), draw in 1-inch decking for joists 16 inches on center and 2-inch decking for joists 24 inches on center. This example uses nominal ¾-inch decking, which is actually 1 inch thick.

This boardwalk design includes a trim board. To indicate it, measure down from the decking the width of the trim board (2½ inches in this design) and draw a line. Then, draw vertical lines at the ends and at each section of the boardwalk.

The final element in the elevation drawing is the boardwalk support. In my design, 6×6 sleepers (horizontal members) are located at the ends of the boardwalk and centered beneath where the sections meet. The boardwalk is raised above the ground 2 or 3 inches, so a portion of the 6×6 support is buried; indicate the buried portion with dashes.

Draw the gravel base to the proper width and depth. To provide adequate support for the 6×6 sleepers, the base should be at least 18 inches wide and 12 inches longer than the sleepers (6 inches at each end); see illustration on page 162. See the box on page 165 to determine the depth of the base and how to estimate the amount of base material that's required. When the drawing is complete, add the dimensions.

Using the plan and elevation drawings, create a materials list, get what you need, and build the boardwalk.

An elevation drawing helps you see proportional relationships, in this case between trim size and the depth of the joists and decking (not visible). ▪

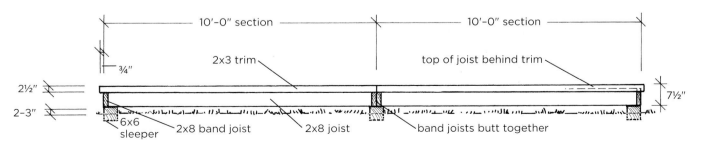

10'-0" section   10'-0" section

¾"
2x3 trim   top of joist behind trim

2½"

2-3"   7½"

6x6 sleeper   2x8 band joist   2x8 joist   band joists butt together

ELEVATION

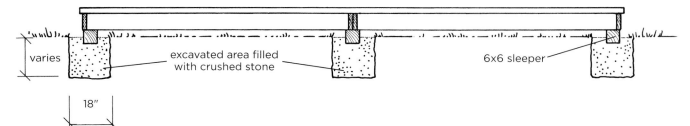

varies

18"

excavated area filled
with crushed stone

6x6 sleeper

For the sleeper to be properly
supported, the crushed-stone
base should extend beyond it by
6" in all directions. A solid base
minimizes movement of the
boardwalk over time, helping it
to stay level and true.

CONSTRUCTING A BOARDWALK

You can compile your own list of materials, but the one provided is a
good starting point. Read carefully through the construction sequence so
you fully understand it.

I recommend building boardwalks in short sections. That way, construction can take place off-site, and each section can easily be trans-
ported to the site. Repairs are also easier when short sections are used.

Materials

½ cubic yard crushed stone or processed gravel for the base
   (18" hole depth)

3 6"x6"x4' pressure-treated (for ground contact) or composite
   plastic timbers

12 feet ½" (#4) rebar, cut into six 2' sections

64 linear feet 2"x6" joist, band joist, and blocking material

240 linear feet ¾" decking material

48 feet 1"x3" trim material for edges (if included)

Rust-resistant (stainless-steel, galvanized, or ceramic-coated)
   decking screws

18 wooden stakes, bracing material, and miscellaneous nails
   (8d, 12d, 16d)

Marking paint or lime

Wood preservative and applicator to treat cut ends

Tools

Circular saw or handsaw

Drill/driver

Driver bit for decking screws

⁹⁄₁₆"x6" drill bit for sleeper anchors

⅛"x2½" drill bit for predrilling decking

Framing square

Hand tamper

Level

Line level, if needed to keep sections even

Marking pencil

Mason's string

Shovel

Sledgehammer

Lay Out the Boardwalk

On the ground, locate the precise position of the boardwalk, including its width and overall length. Place a temporary stake at one corner (stake 1), measure out the 20-foot length of the boardwalk, and install another stake (stake 2). Then measure out the width of the boardwalk (4 feet in this design) and install a third stake (stake 3). Pull a string from stake to stake and use a framing square to confirm that the corner is square.

Next, using two tape measures, measure out 4 feet from stake 2 and 20 feet from stake 3 and place a fourth stake where the tapes intersect (stake 4). Measure the lengths of the diagonals between the opposite stakes to confirm that everything is square. If it is, the lengths of the diagonals should be equal; if not, adjust the stakes until they are (see Keeping Things Square on page 36).

These stakes provide a footprint for the boardwalk, but they must be removed prior to excavation and construction. Set eight offset stakes about 3 or 4 feet away from each corner stake. Then install intermediate stakes where sections of the boardwalk will butt against each other. You'll use these points of reference to reestablish the positions of the corner stakes and the sleepers after the bases have been excavated.

After you have installed the eight offset stakes (stakes 5–12), install two intermediate stakes (stakes 13 and 14) at the midpoint (10' in this design), where the middle sleeper will be installed. ▨

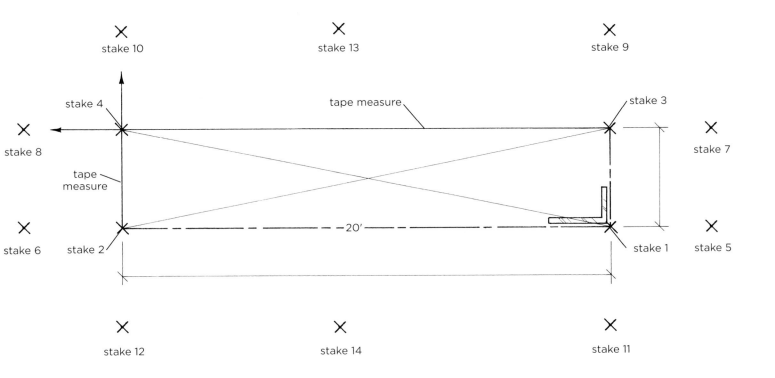

Prepare the Supports: Excavate the Base

The boardwalk supports consist of two parts: a base and a sleeper. The bases are compacted crushed stone or gravel and the sleepers are 6×6 wood or composite plastic timbers. Remove the corner stakes and pull strings from the offset stakes to locate each base. Then, using the dimensions from the elevation drawing, measure out and stake the bases on the ground. Excavate the holes, then line them with landscape fabric to help maintain their integrity (the holes are 1 foot 6 inches deep and 5 feet long in this design).

Boardwalks are constructed to follow the pitch of the ground and to remain a relatively consistent distance above it. When the ground is fairly level, you can level the boardwalk by making minor adjustments to the height of the sleepers. Work methodically, backfilling each hole and setting sleepers individually.

Backfill the first hole with crushed stone or gravel, compacting it every 2 to 4 inches with a hand tamper until you reach the appropriate height.

In this design, the top of the sleeper and bottom of the boardwalk are 3 inches above the ground; the hole is filled to approximately 2½ inches below grade. To keep the supports and boardwalk in a consistent horizontal plane, pull a string from a stake set to 3 inches above the ground (see the illustration on page 166).

This view shows the width of the boardwalk, sleeper, and base. If the decking will overhang the frame, make the frame 3'-10" wide, instead of 4' wide, to account for a 1" overhang on each side. ▪

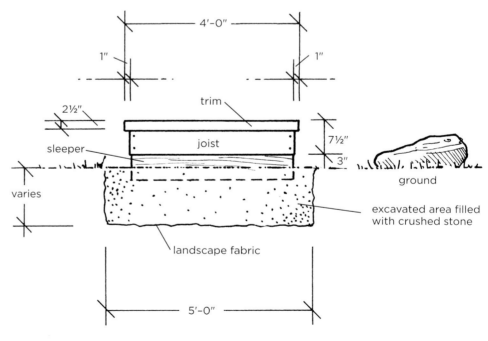

FRONT ELEVATION

How Deep a Base?

This boardwalk is supported by a base of crushed stone or gravel. The appropriate depth of the base depends on the soil type and whether you live in an area where the ground freezes. The goal is to minimize heaving and soil movement that freezing can cause, not to eliminate it completely. Bases 6 inches to 24 inches deep are usually adequate, but local conditions may require a deeper base.

To estimate the amount of gravel that's required, multiply the length by the width by the depth of the hole (in feet). The result is the total number of cubic feet you need; divide that number by 27 to determine cubic yards. Order slightly more gravel than you think you need to be sure you will have plenty.

Prepare the Supports: Set Sleepers

Cut all the sleepers to length (4 feet in this design) at the same time. Drill two 9/16-inch holes about 6 inches in from each end.

Lay the sleeper on the base so it is aligned with the layout strings and level across the width of the boardwalk. When the top of the sleeper is at the correct height (3 inches above the ground in this design) and level, drive 2-foot lengths of #4 rebar through the prepared holes and into the ground. Alternatively, secure the sleepers with 2×4 pressure-treated stakes. Double-check that the sleeper is level before setting the next support.

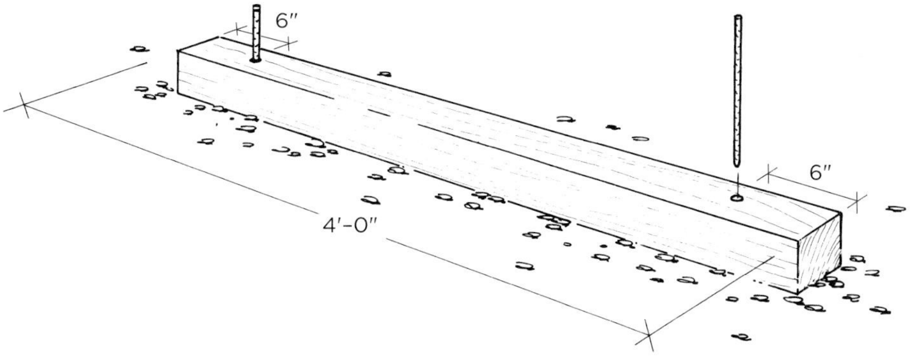

> **TIP**
>
> To prevent weeds and grass from growing under a boardwalk, clear the area of plant growth, install a layer of landscape fabric, and cover it with washed stone.

After securing the sleeper with stakes or rebar (shown here), check it for level and confirm that it is properly aligned with the other sleepers. If it's off significantly, remove it, rework the base, and reset it.

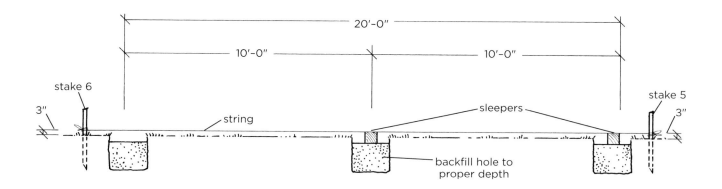

Next, backfill the second hole to proper depth, measure out the required distance from the first to the second sleeper (10 feet in this design), and set the second sleeper on the base. Measure from the outside face of the first sleeper to the center of the second; when the distance is correct, level the sleeper side to side. Check the diagonals, measuring from the ends of the sleepers, to make sure they are square to each other. Then install the rebar, double-check for accuracy, and move on to the last sleeper.

Backfill the last hole with gravel and install the sleeper. Remove the horizontal guide string when you backfill the hole, then replace it to check the alignment of the sleeper. Check the diagonals.

Build the Boardwalk Frames

When the prep work is complete, framing can begin. First, cut the band joists to the width of the bridge (4 feet in this design) and mark them with the appropriate on-center spacing (16 inches in this design). Then cut the joists to the proper length, taking into account the thickness of the band joists. For example, if the band joists are 1½ inches thick and a bridge section is 10 feet long, the joists should be cut to 9 feet 9 inches. It's always a good idea to double-check measurements before making a cut.

Next, position the joists crown up between the band joists and screw or nail them in place. When each frame is complete, carry it to the site and set it on the appropriate sleeper.

TIP

It may seem more logical to build the frames in place on top of the sleepers, but don't. The requisite hammering, banging, pushing, and pulling are apt to knock the sleepers out of level and alignment. A better building site is a firm, level surface such as a driveway or garage floor where tools and power are nearby.

Working with Lumber

Unlike steel or plastic, wood is not a uniform material; each piece is different. Of course, that's part of its charm, but it can also be cause for frustration. Lumber is rarely straight; it may warp, bow, twist, or crown. A piece of lumber may have one or more visual defects, such as knots, voids, checks, and splits. Additionally, the manufacturing process is not always precise: the ends of lumber may not be square, or the lumber may taper in thickness or width from one end to the other.

Inspecting each piece of wood before you cut and build with it will save you time, reduce errors, and result in a better finished project.

To check for a bow or a crown, sight down the width or the length of each piece of lumber, respectively. In a framework, crowns should always be up. To instantly know how a board should be placed during construction, draw an arrow on its side pointing up to the crown; boards will be placed arrow up. Don't use boards with large crowns that might be uneven with the others.

To straighten a bowed decking board, screw one end of the board in place with the bow facing toward the previously installed board. Put a spacer at the next joist, pull the board up to it, and screw it in place. Continue in this manner until the board is installed.

Twisted joists can be difficult to install. If the twist is not too severe, nail the bottom of the joist in place and push against the top until it lines up with the on-center mark, then nail the top in place. Don't use boards if the twist is too great to take out.

Even though most pieces of wood have defects, one face or one side of the board is usually more presentable than the other. In joists and framing lumber, appearance is generally not an issue, except when pieces will be visible on the exterior of the framework. Decking boards should be installed with the best faces up. While inspecting lumber for defects, mark boards with a large X to indicate the less desirable side, and don't expose it during construction.

Attach Frame to Sleepers

First, confirm that the frame is level side to side. Even if the sleeper is level, due to the irregularities of lumber, the frame may not be. If it's slightly off, shim it with wooden shim shingles. If the frame is so out of level that shimming it lifts the frame off the sleeper by more than ¼ inch, adjust the sleeper.

Next, square the frame. To begin, line up one end of the frame with the edge and ends of the sleeper and tack it into place with small nails. Then move to the other end of the frame and align it in the same way. Measure the diagonals. If the diagonals are equal in length, the frame is square. If the diagonals are not equal, release the tacked end and adjust the frame until they are. Make minor adjustments to both sides and ends of the frame to keep it from hanging off the sleepers too much.

When the frame is squared, use decking screws on the inside of each joist bay to attach it to the sleepers. (For more on squaring, see Keeping Things Square on page 36.)

TIP

Straighten a bowed decking board by securing one end, then pulling or prying the problem board tight against the spacer and securing it. Continue working this way until you reach the end of the board.

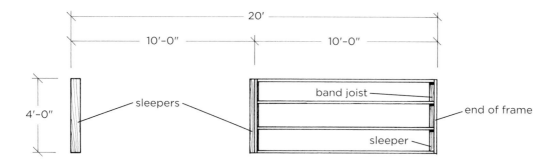

Straighten and Block the Joists

The joists may not be straight, and this can cause problems later. Sight down the frame to look for bowed joists. To straighten the joists, set up a string with spacing blocks along the length of one of the outside joists (see illustration below). Next, put a stake in the ground near the middle of one frame, about 3 to 4 feet away, and nail a 2×3 or 2×4 brace to it. Using a third spacing block at the middle, push or pull the outside joist until the spacing to the string along its length is consistent, then tack the brace to the joist. Finally, tack a 1× brace to the joist that was just straightened. Push or pull each remaining joist until it is correctly spaced and tack it in place through the brace; check spacing with a tape measure.

Boardwalk sections longer than 8 feet also need to be blocked at their middles, between the joists, to help stiffen the frame. Snap a line at the middle of the frame and measure each individual piece of blocking. Cut blocking to length and install it, placing it alternately on either side of the line. Blocking can be nailed, but it's better to screw it in place to avoid shifting the alignment of the frame.

Calculate Decking Spacing

The goal in this step is to ensure the decking pattern ends with a full-width board. Three-eighth-inch spacing is an excellent choice for

When the first frame is square, use decking screws on the inside of each joist bay to attach it to the sleepers. Then position the second frame, square it, and fasten it to the sleepers. Last, screw together the two middle joists.

Straighten the joists to ensure that the outer edges of the decking boards run straight and true.

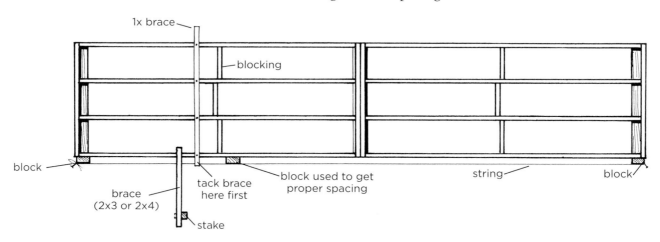

boardwalk decking, so we'll use that measurement as a variable in our calculation. The results of the calculation will determine whether, and to what extent, the spaces need be adjusted. It is possible that the spacing won't work out to a full board. In such a case, overhangs can be adjusted or a few boards may need to be cut (see tip).

In this design, the first and last decking boards are installed flush with the frame. To determine the number of boards needed, measure the length of the boardwalk, then divide that number by the width of the boards plus the anticipated space:

$$\text{no. of boards} = 240 \text{ inches} \div (3\tfrac{1}{2} \text{ inches} + \tfrac{3}{8} \text{ inch})$$
$$= 240 \text{ inches} \div 3\tfrac{7}{8} \text{ inches (or 3.875 inches)}$$
$$= 61.935$$

Because the result is so close to 62, ⅜-inch spacing should work fine. To double-check, round the result to the nearest whole board and multiply by board width:

$$62 \times 3\tfrac{1}{2} \text{ inches} = 217 \text{ inches}$$

Subtract this number from the length of the boardwalk:

$$240 \text{ inches} - 217 \text{ inches} = 23 \text{ inches}$$

Divide this number by the number of spaces (always one less than the number of boards) to confirm the width of the space:

$$23 \text{ inches} \div 61 = \tfrac{3}{8} \text{ inch}$$

Any discrepancies can be addressed by adjusting the position of the last few boards or by adding equally to the planned overhang on each end.

What Spacing Is Best?

The space between decking boards should be small enough that things don't fall through the cracks and large enough that it doesn't hold debris and make cleaning difficult. A ⅜-inch space is ideal.

Two caveats: First, wood decking shrinks and may even swell if the conditions are right. So, even if you start out with a ⅜-inch space, you may end up with one that is slightly larger or smaller. The amount of change depends on the width, moisture content, and species of the board. When you purchase decking, ask the supplier what can be expected and plan accordingly. Second, wood decking is rarely exactly the same width. As you install boards, check spacing by measuring to the end of the frame periodically, and correct discrepancies as you work.

DECKING WITH OVERHANG

If the decking overhangs the frame, the calculation is similar, but first you must add the amount of the overhangs — for example, 1 inch on each side — to the bridge length:

$$\text{no. of boards} = (240 \text{ inches} + 2 \text{ inches}) \div 3\tfrac{7}{8} \text{ (or 3.875) inches}$$
$$= 62.45 \text{ boards}$$

Round the result to the nearest whole board, and multiply it by board width ($62 \times 3\tfrac{1}{2}$). Subtract the result from the total length to calculate the total space in inches ($242 - 217 = 25$ inches). Using a fraction-capable calcutator, divide this number by the number of spaces (one less than the number of boards) to confirm the width of the space ($25 \div 61 = \tfrac{13}{32}$ inch, or $\tfrac{1}{32}$ inch more than $\tfrac{3}{8}$ inch [$\tfrac{1}{32} + \tfrac{12}{32} = \tfrac{13}{32}$]). Use a $\tfrac{13}{32}$ drill bit as a spacer. If you don't have a fraction-capable calculator, refer to a decimal-to-fraction conversion chart, which will show you the $\tfrac{13}{32}$ is the closest equivalent for 0.41.

Preparing Decking Boards

Measure the exact width of the frame and cut a board to the correct length (4 feet in this design). See if it spans the frame appropriately at different spots along the boardwalk. If it does, use this board as a template for the other pieces. If not, measure any spots where the pattern was too long or too short and cut boards to the needed length(s).

Predrill pilot holes for easy screw installation. To create a layout for the holes, take the template to the boardwalk frame and mark the center of the joists on the face of the board, being sure to align it properly. With a square, draw a horizontal line across the board at these points, measure in $\tfrac{1}{2}$ inch from each edge, and drill the holes. Using this piece as a template, mark the other boards and drill the holes.

Install Decking Boards

You're now ready to install the decking boards.

When all the boards are prepared, move the first board into position at the beginning of the boardwalk, flush with the framework, and screw it in place. (If the decking will overhang the ends and sides, use a spacing block that is the thickness of the overhang when positioning the boards.) Next, insert spacers, then position the second board, making sure it is properly aligned with the sides of the framework; screw it into place. Continue working until you've installed all boards.

Decking Tips

- Place the best-looking side of the board face up.
- Treat the undersides of decking boards with preservative before they are installed.
- Predrill pilot holes. For some types of materials — harder woods and composites, for example — this is essential. Even in softer woods, particularly at the ends of boards, predrilling makes screws easier to drive and less likely to cause splitting.
- Secure decking boards with screws; screws hold better than nails and can be removed if necessary.
- Use two screws at each joist and keep the placement pattern regular. Make sure the screws are at least ½ inch in from the edges of the board.
- For consistent spacing, use spacers the same thickness as the desired space. Put spacers between the boards to guide the installation of each board; drill bits of the appropriate size work well.
- Check measurements frequently to ensure that all is going as planned and that the boards are perpendicular to the frame. Frequent checks allow you to correct any discrepancies over several boards rather than all at once. Measure from the ends of each decking board to the end of the frame; the dimensions should be the same.

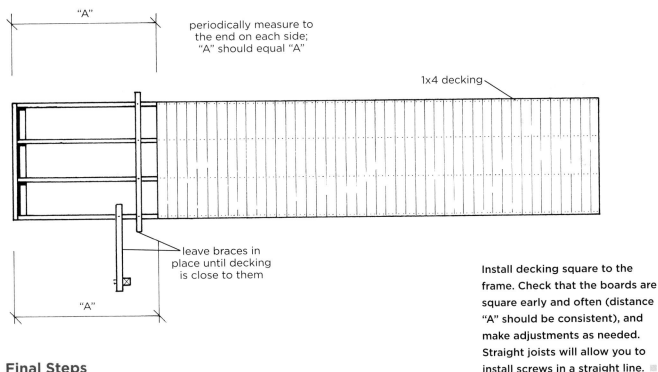

"A"

periodically measure to the end on each side; "A" should equal "A"

1x4 decking

leave braces in place until decking is close to them

"A"

Install decking square to the frame. Check that the boards are square early and often (distance "A" should be consistent), and make adjustments as needed. Straight joists will allow you to install screws in a straight line.

Final Steps

Measure and cut the 1×3-inch trim, and install it with screws. Treat the boardwalk with a preservative or other finish. (See Finishing Touches on page 221.)

The Joisted Bridge and the Simple-Truss Bridge

I will walk you through the construction of a 12-foot joisted bridge and a 20-foot 3-inch truss bridge, both of which are designed to span a small stream. A joisted bridge is relatively straightforward compared to a truss bridge, which may be challenging for the beginning do-it-yourselfer.

If you want to modify the plans provided for either bridge, first choose the site; determine the span, width, and access step height; and decide on a railing style. Additional design information is given below for each bridge type. Otherwise, after reading the introductory material, turn to page 175 for the joisted bridge and to page 196 for construction of the simple-truss bridge. For help sketching out your ideas and making a plan, see Creating Your Own Design on page 147.

Site

Location is important. When reviewing potential sites, consider the approach to the bridge, what the bridge will look like, and what kind of view the bridge will offer.

The approach leading to the bridge sets a mood and deserves careful thought. You can reveal the entrance to the walker or conceal it behind plantings. A winding path to a hidden entrance creates a wonderful sense of anticipation.

Think about how the bridge will be viewed when you site it. Experiment with different locations by putting tall stakes at the corners of a potential bridge site, then look at it from various vantage points.

Last, think about what you will see when standing on the bridge. Shifting the bridge slightly one way or the other, upstream or downstream, can open up unexpected views or provide needed privacy. Create a temporary "viewing" bridge by laying an aluminum extension ladder across the stream from bank to bank and then running a couple of planks across it.

Span

Once you know the location of the bridge, you need to determine how far the bridge will span. If the bridge will span a stream or gully, its length is determined by the width of the obstacle. If you'll use the bridge only decoratively, choose a span that works with the design of the landscape.

Width

The width of a bridge is determined primarily by how it will be used and the number of people expected to cross it simultaneously. For example, a

Joisted and simple-truss bridge width

WIDTH	WALKING PATTERN	ACTIVITY
3' to 4'	Single file	Wide enough for carrying packages
4 'to 5'	Two people abreast	Adequate for wheelbarrow or carrying bulky items
5' and wider	Two people can pass easily	Frequent use by walkers going back and forth

small bridge in a private garden might be wide enough for only one person to cross at a time. On the other hand, a working bridge should be wide enough to accommodate a wheelbarrow.

Use the information supplied in the chart to help you select the width that will work for your needs. Width dimensions are somewhat subjective, so it's a good idea to try to find, walk on, and measure bridges of different widths to determine the width you feel will suit your purposes.

Access Height

The height of the bridge relative to the ground is another important design decision. When determining access height, consider how the bridge will be used and its setting. To make a garden bridge more visible, you might want to build it up with one or more steps. But if the bridge will be crossed frequently with a wheelbarrow, it should be flush with the ground. The banks of a stream may not be level with each other, in which case one end of the bridge might have one step while the other has two steps.

Railings, Posts, and Balusters

Of all the bridge components, railings have the greatest impact on the appearance of a bridge. With their nearly endless array of styles, railings can be simple and practical, highly decorative, or anything in between. If you want to encourage lingering, choose a railing that's high enough to lean on. There are so many possibilities that looking at a good number of examples makes sense.

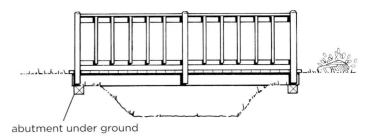

abutment under ground

BRIDGE FLUSH WITH GROUND

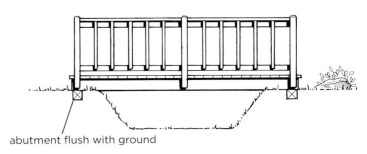

abutment flush with ground

BRIDGE ONE RISER UP

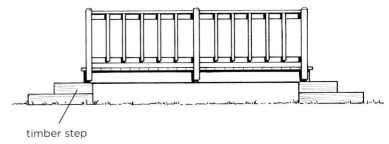

timber step

BRIDGE TWO STEPS UP

Consider how the bridge will be used when determining access height. A bridge deck flush with the ground is unobtrusive and easily accommodates strollers and wheelbarrows, whereas bridges with steps or risers are more pronounced and heighten the sense of arrival. ▪

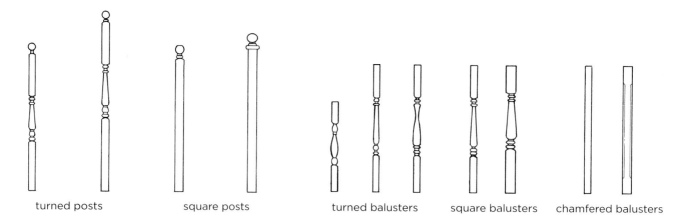

turned posts   square posts   turned balusters   square balusters   chamfered balusters

Posts and balusters are available in a variety of styles and sizes. Study porch railings to get a sense of what you like, and notice how baluster spacing affects the look and feel of a railing. ▪

Posts and balusters also affect the look of a bridge. Square posts and balusters are informal, whereas ornate posts and highly turned balusters are formal. Horizontal rails for bridges are typically made with 2×4 or 2×6 dimension stock and produce simple, clean lines.

Posts and balusters are available in a variety of sizes and styles. Posts can be square or rectangular and their tops flat, beveled, or capped with a ball or other shape. Balusters can be square, rectangular, round, or turned. Choose the look that pleases your eye and suits your purposes.

Railing Safety and Building Codes

Residential footbridges are considered landscape features and therefore are not regulated by national building codes. However, local jurisdictions may have their own regulations, so check with your building inspector to find out if railing and baluster strength and placement are regulated for footbridges.

The building codes in many jurisdictions require porches and decks more than 30 inches above the ground to have guardrails at least 36 inches high. Additionally, the spaces between horizontal balusters and rails are to be no wider than 4 inches. These specifications are meant to prevent small children from going over or through the railing, or getting their heads stuck between the balusters. Follow these recommendations if you want to build your railing "to code."

Codes also specify guardrail strength, as defined by the amount of load, or force, that a guardrail must be able to resist without failing. Because there are myriad railing designs, it's beyond the scope of this book to provide strength information for all of them.

Follow these general guidelines:
- 4×4 posts: set a maximum of 8 feet apart and bolt in place with two ½-inch bolts
- 2×6 top rail for baluster railing system: install flat with a 2×4 sub-rail installed on-edge below it and 2×2 balusters attached to the sub-rail and to the bridge frame (see railing design for the joisted bridge)
- 2×6 top rail and 2×4 intermediate rails for horizontal railing systems: install flat with 2×4 sub-rails installed on-edge below them (see railing design for the simple-truss bridge)
- Toenail or screw the rails to the posts securely. (Nails and screws should pass 1½ inches into the post.)

THE JOISTED BRIDGE

While it's no more difficult than building a small deck, the benefits of building a joisted bridge can be great. A joisted bridge can provide easy access to parts of your property cut off by a gully or stream or add a focal point to your flower garden.

My joisted bridge design is 12 feet long and 4 feet wide. It's set on the ground. If you want to modify the plan provided, first review the general information above (see page 172), then work through the next sections; otherwise, after reading the introductory materials, turn to page 182. For help sketching out your ideas and making a plan, see Creating Your Own Design on page 147.

THE PLANS You need to create an elevation drawing and a framing and decking plan.

Determine Bridge Span and Position of Abutments Refer to your site plan if you have one, then draw the profile of the stream (or obstacle) the bridge will cross. If you don't have a site plan, take measurements from the site. First, measure the bank-to-bank distance of the stream. Next, determine the amount of slope of each bank by plumbing up from the toe of the slope and measuring over to the bank. Then, measure the depth and width of the streambed. Last, determine the relative heights of the banks by using a line level, a 4-foot level on a straight board, or a transit.

A bridge must be longer than the bank-to-bank distance it spans. For reasons of integrity and stability, abutments cannot be placed directly on the edges of the banks. In most situations, positioning abutments 2 to 4 feet back from the bank edge is sufficient, but unstable soils may require even more clearance (see box on page 184). Indicate the width and depth of the base on your drawing, then draw the abutments.

The Elevation Drawing With the span and abutments set, draw the frame. Refer to the span chart on page 177 and pick the joist size and on-center spacing that work for the span of the bridge you want to build. A 12-foot span requires 2×8 joists at 16 inches on center, for example.

As a general rule, the steeper a bank, the farther away from the edge an abutment should be located. If one bank slopes more steeply than the other, as is usually the case, set both abutments at the more conservative distance. ▨

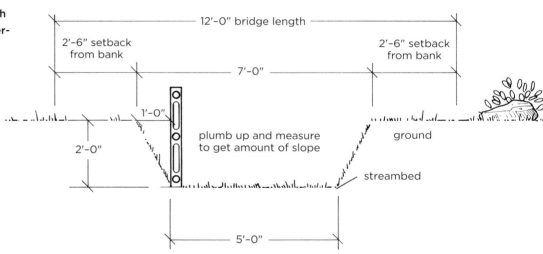

The elevation drawing helps you see how the parts of the bridge relate to each other and to the site as well. ▨

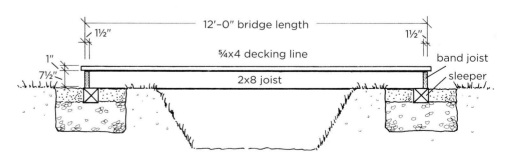

Joist size and spacing

SPAN	ON-CENTER SPACING	NOMINAL SIZE*
6'	24"	2×6
8'	16" to 24"	2×6
10'	16" to 24"	2×8
12'	16"	2×8
12'	24"	2×10
14'	16"	2×10
14'	24"	2×12
16'	16" to 24"	2×12

*Pressure-treated southern yellow pine or Douglas fir.
Note: Plan to install blocking between joists that are 8 feet to 12 feet long; joists longer than 12 feet require blocking at every third of their length and aligned with rail posts.
On-center spacing refers to the distance between the centers of adjacent joists.

Draw the length and width of the joist, then indicate band joists at the ends. The band joists are short boards installed perpendicular to the joists at the ends of the bridge to which the joists are secured. Show the thickness of the band joists (1½ inches in my design).

Next, indicate the thickness of the decking (1 inch actual [¾ inch nominal] in my design), so you can account for it when determining the height of the top rail. If the decking thickness is not known at this time (see page 145 for more on decking thickness), draw in 1-inch decking for joists that are 16 inches on center and 2-inch decking for joists 24 inches on center.

Railings Before designing and drawing the railings, decide on the style you want. In my joisted bridge design, the railings have balusters.

Posts Post layout is important to overall bridge design. It's a matter of aesthetics and safety. (See page 174 for more on safety.)

First determine the post spacing. Experiment with different options by using tracing-paper overlays.

Mark the locations and width of the posts (4×4 nominal in my design) on the frames, drawing them slightly longer than the anticipated finished height of the top rail (3 feet 6 inches in my design). To make installation easier, plan to set the posts in from the end, at least the thickness of the band joist.

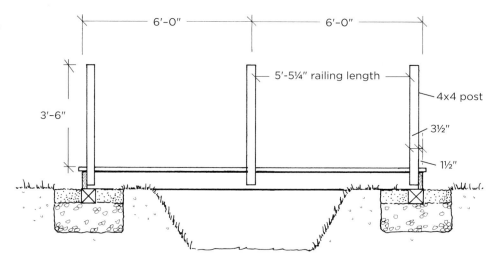

Symmetry is pleasing to the eye, so I chose to use equal, 6' spacing between the posts in my joisted bridge design. ▪

Top Rails There are two basic approaches to attaching railings to posts: post-to-post and over-the-post. With the first method, the posts project above the plane of the top rail. This style tends to stop the eye at the posts, emphasizing the vertical post elements. In contrast, an over-the-post top rail is installed in an unbroken run, over the top of the post, so it emphasizes the horizontal rather than the vertical. (See illustrations on page 146.)

Before settling on a type, experiment with both approaches on paper. Keep in mind that post-to-post systems generally look best if the railings are the same width or narrower than the posts, and the over-the-post version looks better when the top rail is wider than the post.

Post-to-Post Top Rails and Balusters At the desired height (36 inches in my design), draw the top rail and the sub-rail (a 2×4 in my design) in between the posts. The posts project above the top rail and can be one of many styles (see page 174). Choose a style and the height it projects above the top rail, and draw it in.

If you want baluster spacing to conform to building codes, draw them with 4-inch spaces in between. Otherwise, experiment with spacing and choose your favorite. (In my design, there are five balusters, 9⅝ inches apart.) Balusters are available with square, rectangular, or turned cross sections (see page 174); when drawing them, however, just draw simple, square balusters.

To calculate the precise baluster spacing, deduct the total thickness of all the balusters from the railing length. Divide this by the number of spaces, which is always one more than the number of balusters, to get the width of each space.

width of each space = (railing length – total baluster thickness) ÷ no. of spaces
(no. of balusters + 1)

$$= (5'\text{-}5\tfrac{1}{4}" - 7\tfrac{1}{2}" \; [5 \times 1\tfrac{1}{2}"]) \div (6 \text{ spaces})$$
$$= \text{width of each space } 4'\text{-}9\tfrac{3}{4}" \div 6$$
$$= 9\tfrac{5}{8}"$$

Balusters are secured either directly to the bridge frame or to a bottom rail. While it's faster and easier to attach balusters to the frame, this approach looks less finished. It also presents two unwanted consequences. First, if someone stands close to and leans on the rail, she'll probably bump her toes against the balusters; second, because the balusters are attached to the frame, sweeping the bridge becomes a challenge, especially if balusters are set close together. Securing the balusters to a bottom rail set a few inches above the bridge deck avoids these problems.

After you've decided how you will secure the balusters, mark them out along the length of the frame and draw them in. My design uses a 2×4 bottom rail.

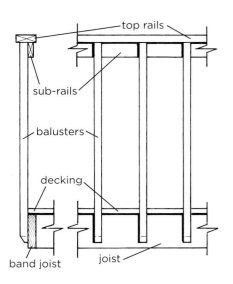

A BALUSTERS ATTACHED TO FRAME

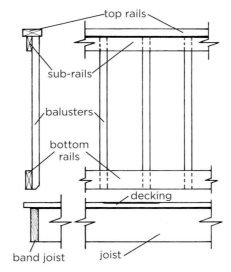

B BALUSTERS ATTACHED TO BOTTOM RAIL

Balusters can be attached to the frame *(A)* or to the bottom rail *(B)*. The former is the easier method of the two, but the latter looks more finished and makes chores like sweeping easy. ▪

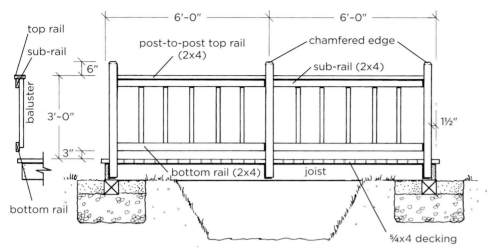

top rail

sub-rail

baluster

bottom rail

6'-0"

6'-0"

post-to-post top rail
(2x4)

chamfered edge

sub-rail (2x4)

6"

3'-0"

3"

1½"

bottom rail (2x4)

joist

¾x4 decking

ELEVATION PLAN

Add crucial dimensions to the completed elevation plan drawing. You'll use this, in conjunction with the framing and decking plans, to compile a materials list. Be sure to order materials for both sides of the bridge. ▪

TIP

In my bridge design, the decking overhangs the sides of the frame by 1 inch. By reducing the width of the bridge by 2 inches, from 4 feet to 3 feet 10 inches, you can use 4-foot decking boards, cutting two from a standard 8-foot length.

Framing and Decking Plan The framing and decking plans help you visualize the bridge from above. Start with the framing plan. First, lightly draw the outline of the frame: the two outside joists and two band joists. Next, fill in the remaining joists (16-inch on-center spacing is used in my design). Remember that joist spacing is a function of span and decking thickness; for guidelines, see the chart on page 177 and the information on page 145. After indicating all joists, draw in the blocking, darken the drawing, and add dimensions to the plan. The completed drawing is the framing plan.

Tape a piece of tracing paper over the framing plan, then draw the decking plan. First locate and draw the posts. The 4×4 posts (3½×3½ inches actual size) are notched at the bottom to accommodate the thickness of the joists (1½ inches in my design). See page 68 for an explanation of *notching*.

Then, make a series of marks equal to the width of the decking boards (4 inches in my design), including the ⅜-inch space between boards, along one side of the bridge. Draw each board individually and account for the 1-inch overhang at the frame. Darken your lines, add dimensions, and indicate the location of the posts. If the decking doesn't end with a full-width board, don't worry about it now. We'll address that when the boards are installed. You don't need to draw the top rail. When all the boards are drawn in, the decking plan is finished.

When drawing the framing plan, work from the outside in: draw band and outer joists first, then interior joists and blocking.

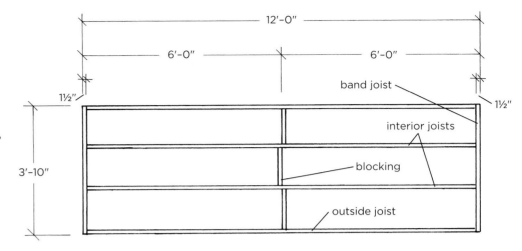

12'-0"

6'-0"   6'-0"

1½"   1½"

band joist

interior joists

blocking

outside joist

3'-10"

FRAMING PLAN

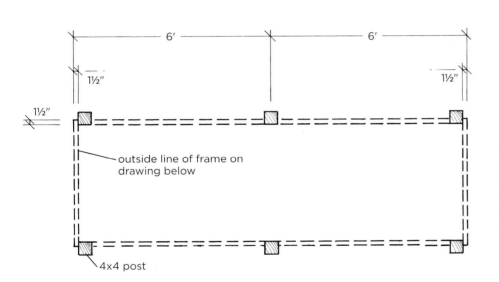

6'   6'

1½"   1½"

1½"

outside line of frame on drawing below

4x4 post

The inside faces of the posts should align with the inner edge of the joists. Posts are most easily attached to the frame if set in from the end at least the width of the band joist, 1½" in my design.

It's nice when decking ends with a full-width board and no cuts are needed. See page 190 to learn how to calculate decking spacing.

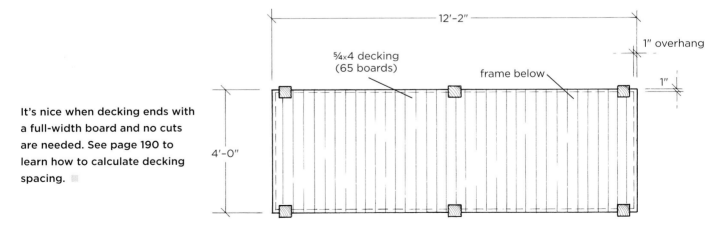

12'-2"

1" overhang

⁵⁄₄x4 decking
(65 boards)

frame below

1"

4'-0"

DECKING PLAN

CONSTRUCTING A JOISTED BRIDGE

You can compile your own materials list, but the one provided is a good start. Before you begin to build, read carefully through the construction sequence.

Materials

Abutments

- 100 square feet landscape fabric (approximately 13′ of a 6′ wide roll) for base
- 2 cubic yards crushed stone or gravel for base
- 2   6″x6″x8′ pressure-treated (for ground contact) or composite timbers for sleepers
- 8 feet, ½″ (#4) rebar, cut into four 2′ sections

Bridge

- 18 wooden stakes, bracing material, and an assortment of nails (8d, 12d, 16d)
- Marking paint or lime
- 64 linear feet 2″x8″ joist, band joist, and blocking material
- 26 linear feet 4″x4″ posts
- 148 linear feet ⁵⁄₄″x4″ decking stock
- 80 linear feet 2″x4″ top and bottom rail, and sub-rail stock
- 52 linear feet 2″x2″ baluster stock
- 12   ½″x4½″ galvanized or stainless-steel carriage bolts, washers, and nuts to attach posts
- #8-size stainless-steel, ceramic-coated, or galvanized decking screws

Tools

- Circular saw
- Drill
- ⅛″x2½″ drill bit for predrilling decking
- ⁹⁄₁₆″x7″ drill bit for sleeper anchors
- Framing square
- Handsaw
- Hand tamper
- Line level, 4′ level and straight board, or transit
- Marking paint or lime
- Mason's string
- Shovel
- Sledgehammer

Lay Out Abutments

Locate the precise position of the bridge on the site.

To begin, install a temporary stake (stake 1) at one end of the bridge, measure out the length of the bridge, and install another stake (stake 2). Then measure out from the first stake the width of the bridge and install a third stake (stake 3). Pull a string from each stake and use a framing square to confirm that the corner is square. Adjust if it's not.

Next, using two tape measures, measure out the width of the bridge from stake 2 and the length of the bridge from stake 3 and place a fourth stake where the tapes intersect (stake 4). Measure the lengths of the diagonals between the opposite stakes to confirm that everything is square. The diagonals should be equal; if not, adjust the stakes until they are (see Keeping Things Square on page 36).

These four stakes mark the corners of the bridge; however, during construction they will be removed. Using strings as a guide, install offset stakes 3 or 4 feet away from the corner stakes so you'll be able to re-establish their position after the base has been excavated. These will also be used to locate and set the position of the bases and sleepers.

Before excavating holes for the bases, establish the elevation, or height above the ground, of the finished bridge. In this design, the bottom of the bridge is level with the ground. This requires a single riser up to the bridge. At stake 5, measure up from the ground the depth of the bridge frame (7½ inches in this design) and put a mark on the stake. Then, using a line level, level-on-board, or transit, transfer that mark to each of the offset stakes.

Remove the corner stakes (stakes 1–4) and mark out the 2-foot 6-inch by 5-foot base using marking paint or lime. Remove the guide strings so they aren't in the way during excavation.

Accurate staking and guide strings help ensure that the base and sleepers will be square and parallel to each other. Offset stakes (stakes 5–10) help you to reestablish the position of the corner stakes (stakes 1–4) after excavation. ▪

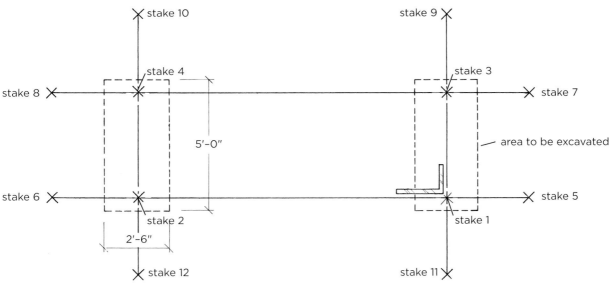

About Abutments

This joisted footbridge is a single span that carries relatively small, predictable loads. Accordingly, it is supported by a simple abutment: a *sleeper,* or 6×6 pressure-treated or composite plastic landscape timber and a base. Sleepers are set directly on the gravel or crushed-stone base and installed perpendicular to the length of the bridge.

An easy and effective way to build steps leading up to a bridge is to incorporate them into the design of the abutment. For example, timbers can be added to create one or more steps, or even a landing (see chapter 5, Steps, for more information on how to build steps).

To ensure that the bridge is adequately and uniformly supported, and to facilitate the installation and alignment of the sleeper, plan a base that is 2 feet 6 inches wide and 12 inches longer than the sleeper. The base must extend 6 inches beyond steps in all directions to provide adequate support.

The appropriate depth of the base depends on the soil type and the depth of the frost line. The goal is to minimize excessive movement, not necessarily to eliminate it. Bases between 6 inches and 24 inches deep are usually adequate, but deeper bases may be needed in the coldest regions.

The bridge also can be supported on concrete foundations installed below the frost line. If you want to build this type of support, seek professional assistance.

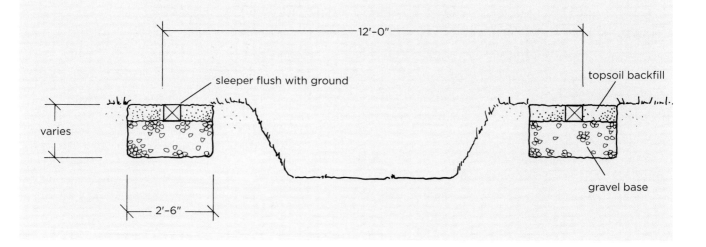

Install Abutments

Excavate the holes (see How Deep a Base on page 165 for guidelines), then line them with landscape fabric to help maintain their integrity.

Backfill with crushed stone or gravel and use a hand tamper to compact it every 2 to 4 inches. When backfilling, keep in mind the thickness of the sleeper, the thickness of the joist, and the desired elevation of the finished bridge. In this design, I've allowed 5½ inches at the top of the hole for the sleeper, so when set, it's flush with the ground. The top of the bridge is 7½ inches above that, the depth of the joist.

Next, cut sleepers to the exact width of the bridge (3 feet 10 inches in this design). Measure in 6 inches from each end of the sleeper and drill a ⁹⁄₁₆-inch hole.

Set the height of the bases with a level string drawn between two stakes, or with a builder's level or transit. Slight adjustments to the base height may be necessary when the sleepers are installed.

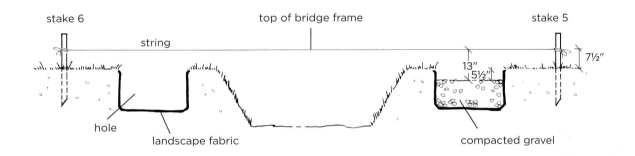

The sleepers are secured with 2′ lengths of rebar. Driving the rebar through the sleepers may disturb them, so before installing the frame, double-check the sleepers to confirm they are square and level; make needed adjustments.

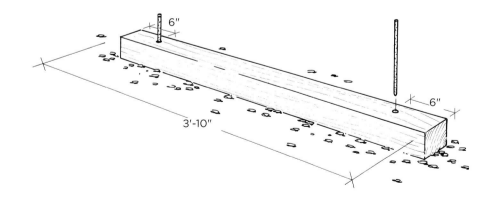

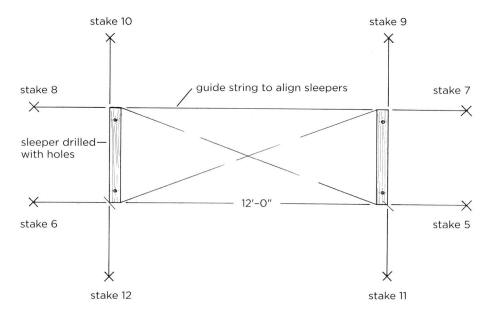

stake 10

stake 9

stake 8

guide string to align sleepers

stake 7

sleeper drilled— with holes

12'-0"

stake 6

stake 5

stake 12

stake 11

Use the guide strings to position the sleepers. Use a tape measure to confirm that sleepers are the correct distance apart, 12′ in this design, and square to each other by checking the diagonals. Also confirm that sleepers are level across their lengths and with each other.

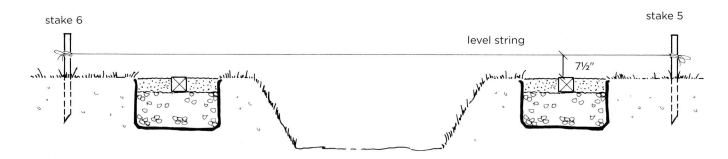

stake 6

stake 5

level string

7½"

Pull strings from the offset stakes to reestablish the exact locations of the sleepers, then set them in position. They must be square with each other and level across the width and length of the bridge. Check diagonal measurements, which should be equal; adjust if necessary. If the sleeper isn't level, add or remove base material to level it. When you're satisfied that each sleeper is level and in the correct position, drive a 2-foot length of ½-inch (#4) rebar through the holes in the sleeper to secure it.

Build the Frame

Find a firm, level surface on which to build the bridge frame. *Never* work right on top of the sleepers; pounding can knock them out of alignment. The completed joisted bridge frame should be easy for two people to carry to the site. Before beginning construction, read Working with Lumber on page 167.

The frame for this joisted bridge design is 12 feet long and 3 feet 10 inches wide. Cut band joists to the width of the frame, then mark them for the appropriate on-center spacing (16 inches in this design). Cut the joists to the proper length, taking into account the thickness of the band joists. Each band joist is 1½ inches thick; therefore, the joists should be 11 feet 9 inches long. Double-check your measurements before cutting.

Position the joists crown up between the band joists and screw or nail them into place. When the frame is complete, carry it to the site and set it on the sleepers.

SQUARE AND ATTACH FRAME

The frame must be squared before you secure it to the sleepers (see Keeping Things Square on page 36). To begin, line up one end of the frame with the side and ends of the sleeper and tack it in place with small nails. Then move to the opposite end of the bridge and align it as you did the first. Measure the diagonals. If they're equal, the frame is square. If they're not, release the tacked end and adjust the frame until they are. Make minor adjustments to both sides and ends of the frame to keep any discrepancies with the sleeper even. When the frame is squared, attach it to the sleepers at each joist bay with a #8 decking screw.

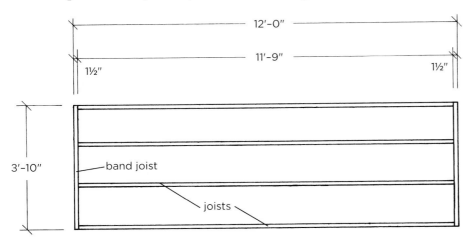

A garage floor or level driveway is a good place to build the bridge frame. Cut and install the outer joists first, then the inner ones; always install joists crown-side up.

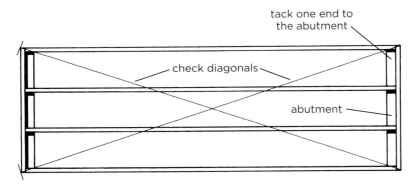

Before squaring the frame, check to see that its width and length are level. If not, determine the source of the problem and shim the frame on the sleepers or adjust the sleepers.

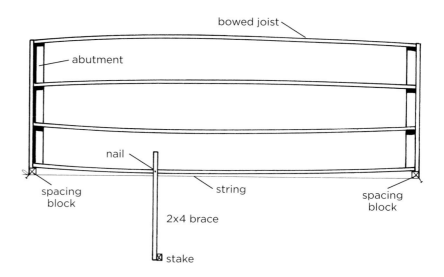

bowed joist

abutment

nail

string

spacing block

spacing block

2x4 brace

stake

Straighten the joists to ensure that the outer edges of the decking boards run straight and true and that overhangs are consistent.

Straighten the Frame

Next, true the joists. Straighten joists by setting up a guide string, with spacing blocks, along the outer joist or bottom chord. Place a stake in the ground near the middle of the frame (avoid post locations), about 5 or 6 feet away, and nail a 2×4 brace to it. Then, using a third spacing block at the middle, push or pull the outside joist until the space to the string is consistent. Tack the brace to the joist. Last, tack a 1× brace to the joist that was just straightened. Push or pull the remaining joists until they are spaced correctly (use a tape measure to check measurements) and tack them in place through the brace.

Install Blocking

First, review the span chart on page 177 for required blocking. Installing blocking between the joists helps stiffen the frame. Snap a line at the blocking locations and measure the length for each piece of blocking. Cut blocking to length, then install it, placing it on alternate sides of the line. Screw blocking in place, don't nail it; hammering can shift the frame out of alignment. If the outer blocking is in line with the position of the railing posts, install the blocking *after* the posts are in place.

Lay Out and Cut the Posts

With a framing square, mark the position of the posts on the outer joists. Next, determine the length of the posts. The planned height of the top rail in this design is 36 inches. To this, add the thickness of the decking (1 inch) and the depth of the joist (7½ inches in this design). Because the design requires the posts to project above the top rail by 6 inches, add that amount to the total post length.

Posts flush with the bottom of the joist are not as appealing visually as those held above it by ½ inch or so. Adjust your calculation accordingly,

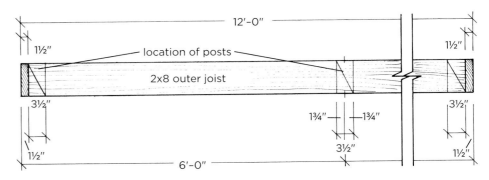

SIDE VIEW

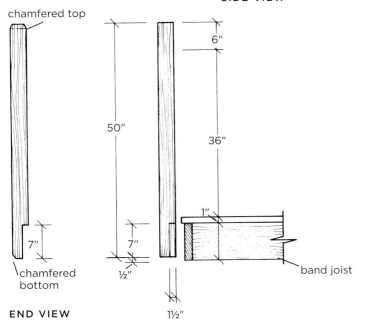

END VIEW

▲ Mark the post locations on both outer joists. To position the middle post precisely, measure and mark the center of the bridge, 6' in this design. Then measure 1¾" on either side of the center line to account for the 3½" width of the post. ▦

◀ The post notch rests directly on the joist. However, be aware that top rail height is measured from the top of the decking, not the top of the joist; the distance from the top of the decking to the top rail is 36" in this design. ▦

then cut the post to length. The posts for this design are 50 inches long.

At the bottom of the post, mark the height of the notch (7 inches [7½ inches – ½ inch] in this design). Set the circular saw to the correct depth (1½ inches) and cut the notch. Use multiple cuts to make the notch, then clean it up with a chisel. This is your test post. Check to see if it's plumb and confirm proper fit and height before notching all the posts. Chamfer top and bottom edges for a finished look.

Attach Posts

Through-bolts provide a stronger connection than lag screws and are the better choice. Good access to the frame makes this step easier.

First, clamp the posts in their proper locations. As you place each post, make sure it's plumb side to side and back and forth and that the top is level with the other posts. Then mark the locations of the holes: they should be at least 1 inch in from the edges of the joist and centered on the post. Remove the posts to predrill two pilot holes, or drill them in

> **TIP**
>
> Install railing posts *before* laying out the decking so you'll have total access when you fit, predrill, and fasten the decking boards.

After the posts bolts are installed, check for plumb one last time, then tighten. If a post is out-of-plumb east to west along the bridge's length, shift the post's position, then retighten the bolts. If a post is out-of-plumb north to south across the bridge's width, you may need to adjust the notches. ▪

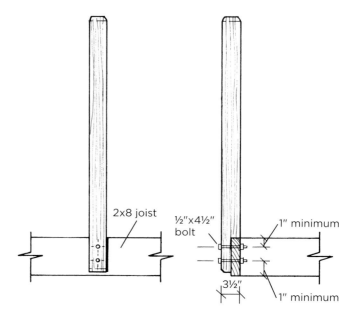

2x8 joist

½"x4½" bolt

1" minimum

3½"

1" minimum

place. The holes must be drilled through the posts and frame to accept ½-inch bolts that are an inch longer than the thickness of the material they will bolt together (4½ inches in this design). Insert the bolts, check to be sure that all is plumb, then tighten the bolts securely.

Add nailers at posts to support the decking when it's notched around the posts. Install the remaining blocking, if necessary.

Calculate Decking Spacing

To be certain the decking pattern ends with a full-width board, plan the layout before you begin installation. First, determine the number of boards needed. Measure the bridge frame, then account for any overhangs. (This bridge is 12 feet long, with a planned 1-inch overhang at each end, or 146 inches.) Divide that number by the width of the decking boards (3½ inches) plus the anticipated space (⅜ inches): 146 ÷ 3⅞ [or 3.875]). Round the result (37.67) to the nearest whole board (38) and multiply it by board width (3½). Subtract this (133 inches) from the total length to calculate the total space in inches (146 − 133 = 13 inches).

Next, determine actual overhang with ⅜-inch spacing between boards. Multiply the number of spaces (one less than the number of boards) by the planned space (37×⅜ inch = 13⅞ inches). Add one half of the excess to each end of the bridge for a ⁷⁄₁₆-inch overhang on each end.

For more information about spacing decking, see page 169.

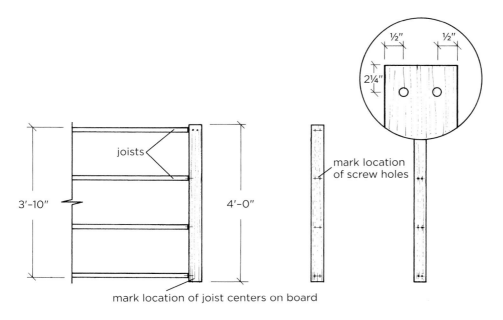

joists

3'-10"

4'-0"

2¼"

½" ½"

mark location of screw holes

mark location of joist centers on board

Creating a template and precutting boards and predrilling pilot holes increases accuracy and speeds up decking installation. Round or chamfer ends of boards with a plane or router. ▪

Install the Decking Boards

Measure the width of the frame, add the amount of overhang at the sides, and cut a board to the correct length (4 feet in this design). Use this board as a template for the remaining decking boards and cut them. Treat the undersides of the boards with preservative.

Predrill pilot holes for easy screw installation. To create a pattern for drilling holes, mark the center of the joists on the face of a board, being sure to allow for the appropriate overhangs. With a square, draw a line across the face of the board, measure in ½ inch from each edge, and drill and countersink to accept the screws. Use this piece to mark screw locations on the other boards, then drill the holes.

When all the boards are prepared, it's a quick job to screw them into place. Position the first board so it has proper overhangs, then install the screws. Move the second board into position and place spacers between the two boards. Make sure the ends of the second board are properly aligned with the ends of the first board and secure the screws. Leave the joist bracing in place until you reach it with the decking.

Continue working in this manner until all boards are installed. When you encounter a post, notch the decking around it. Measure the depth and length of the notch and cut it partway through with a power saw; finish the cut with a handsaw. For more decking tips, see page 171.

TIP

Straighten any bowed decking boards by securing one end, then pulling or prying the problem board tight against the spacer and securing it. Continue working this way until you reach the end of the board.

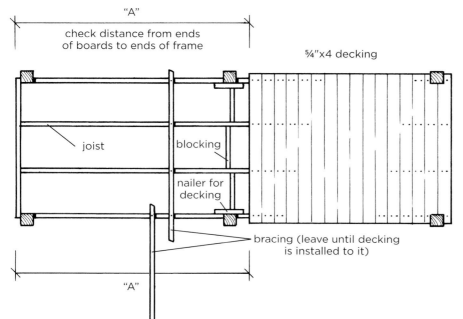

"A"

check distance from ends of boards to ends of frame

⁵⁄₄"x4 decking

joist

blocking

nailer for decking

bracing (leave until decking is installed to it)

"A"

Install decking square to the frame. Check that the boards are square early and often, and make adjustments as needed. The distance from ends of boards to ends of frame ("A") should be consistent. Straight joists will allow you to install screws in a straight line.

Install Post-to-Post Railings with Balusters

Double-check the posts to be sure they are still plumb. If not, bring them back into alignment.

Start by installing the top rail. First, mark the height of the top rail on each post (36 inches in this design). Then determine the length of each rail section. It's most accurate to hold up a piece of railing stock to the posts and mark the length directly than it is to use a tape measure. Draw cut lines on the face of the rail stock with a square and cut it to length.

Hold the cut railing in position — you may need help with this — and screw it into place. Continue individually marking, cutting, and installing the remaining top railings.

It's easy to make a mistake when transferring dimensions to the rail stock with a tape measure. Instead, hold up a piece of railing stock between the posts and mark the length directly.

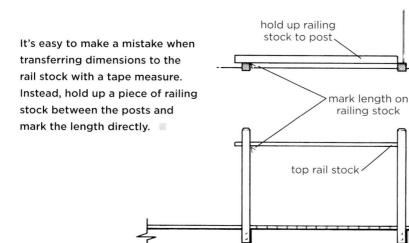

hold up railing stock to post

mark length on railing stock

top rail stock

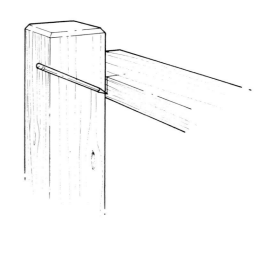

Next prepare and install the sub-rails and bottom rails. As was done for the top rails, measure and cut the sub-rails and bottom rails to length. Then, install the sub-rail directly below the top rail; place it ¼ inch in from the outside edge of the top rail for a more finished look (see bottom illustration, page 194). To locate the bottom rail, measure up from the decking the height of the desired toe space (3 inches in this design) and install the bottom rail, ¼-inch in from the outside edge.

Next, lay out the balusters along the sub-rails, accounting for the thickness of the baluster and the space between each (1½ inches and 9⅝ inches, respectively, in this design). Then, with a level, plumb down and transfer the marks to the bottom rail.

Now, measure and cut the balusters to the proper length (31¼ inches in this design). This creates a ¼-inch reveal at the bottom rail. Dress and finish the balusters: bevel and sand the bottoms. Position balusters at the layout marks and install them one by one, centering the screws on the width of the balusters.

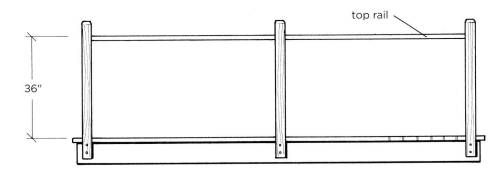

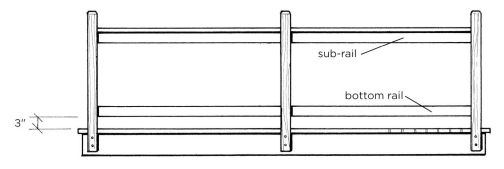

The bridge starts to take shape with the installation of the railing system. Install the top rails first, then the sub-rails, and finally the bottom rails.

On the inner edge of the sub-rail, mark baluster locations. Then, using a level, transfer the marks to the bottom rail. Use the marks to guide installation. ▧

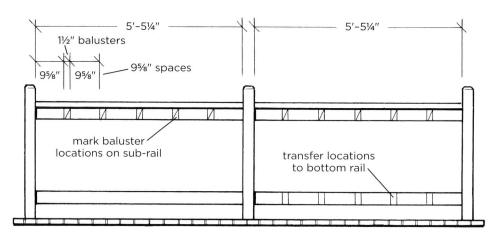

5'–5¼" 5'–5¼"

1½" balusters

9⅝" spaces

9⅝" 9⅝"

mark baluster
locations on sub-rail

transfer locations
to bottom rail

INTERIOR VIEW, DECKING UP

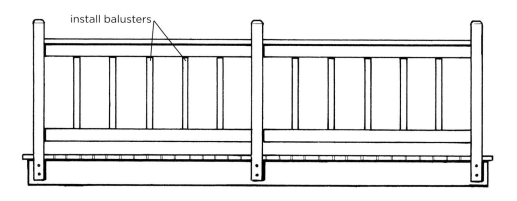

install balusters

EXTERIOR VIEW, JOIST UP

The top rail overhangs the sub-rail and baluster by ¼" on each side, which shields the baluster's end grain from water. ▧

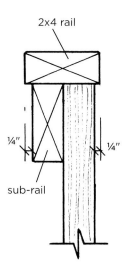

2x4 rail

¼" ¼"

sub-rail

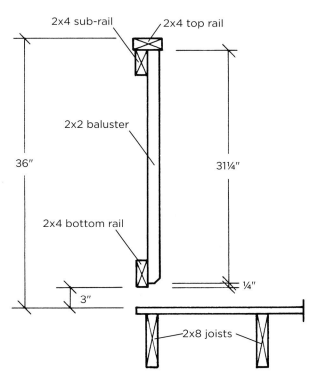

2x4 sub-rail 2x4 top rail

2x2 baluster

36" 31¼"

2x4 bottom rail

¼"

3"

2x8 joists

Finishing Touches

Sand and smooth rough edges and surfaces. Pay particular attention to places that might be prone to splintering. If necessary, glue them with a waterproof glue or nail them in place before they cause problems or get worse.

Apply a sealer or stain to help protect the bridge from the elements. Choose an environmentally friendly, water-based product. You will have to reapply any type of preservative regularly, perhaps yearly, so choose one that is easy to work with.

THE SIMPLE-TRUSS BRIDGE

If you need to span a long distance, want to add a unique feature to your landscape, or would like to test your building skills, the simple-truss bridge is the project for you. My truss bridge design is 20 feet 3 inches long and 4 feet wide.

If you want to modify the plan provided, first review the general information above (see page 172), then work through the next sections; otherwise, after reading the introductory material, turn to page 204. For help sketching out your ideas and making a plan, see Creating Your Own Design on page 147.

THE PLANS You need to create an elevation drawing and a framing and decking plan.

Determine Bridge Span and Position of Abutments Refer to your site plan if you have one, then draw the profile of the stream (or obstacle) the bridge will cross. If you don't have a site plan, take measurements from the site. Measure the bank-to-bank distance of the stream. Next, determine the amount of slope of each bank by plumbing up from the toe of

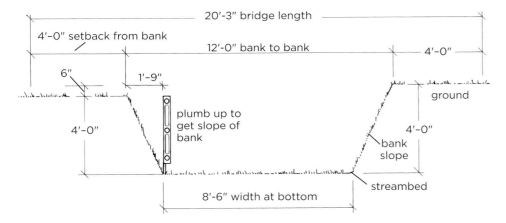

The left bank of this stream is 6" lower than the right. To compensate for this, and to keep the bridge level, the left side of the bridge requires a combination step/sleeper.

the slope and measuring over to the bank. Then, measure the depth and width of the streambed. Last, determine the relative heights of the banks by using a line level, a 4-foot level on a straight board, or a transit.

A bridge must be longer than the bank-to-bank distance it spans. For reasons of integrity and stability, abutments cannot be placed directly on the edges of the banks. In most situations, positioning abutments 2 to 4 feet back from the bank edge is sufficient, but unstable soils may require even more clearance. Indicate the width and depth of the base on your drawing (see box on page 206), then draw the abutments, which include a base and a sleeper.

Elevation Drawing With the span and abutments set, draw the frame. For 12-, 14-, or 16-foot spans with 16- or 24-inch on-center spacing, 2×6s suffice as top and bottom chords for the trusses. The wood is assumed to be pressure-treated southern yellow pine or Douglas fir.

Two of the most important design considerations when planning a simple-truss bridge are pitch and length: specifically, the pitch of the sloped sections of the top chord and the length of the center section of the top chord; both impact the bridge's profile. The slope for my truss bridge design is 3 inches of rise (the vertical distance) for every 12 inches of run (the horizontal distance). The length of the center section of the top chord in my design is 8 feet.

Draw the bottom chord (20 feet long in my design) and then the band joists. Show the thickness of the band joists (1½ inches in my design). Then, along the top of the bottom chord, mark the run of the sloping sections and middle section. (Starting from the inside of the band joints, the sections in my example measure 6 feet, 8 feet, and 6 feet.)

TIP

Err on the side of caution. If you have any doubts about what is required at your site, consult a civil engineer.

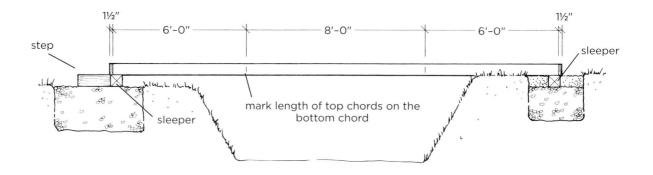

step

sleeper

sleeper

mark length of top chords on the
bottom chord

1½"   6'-0"   8'-0"   6'-0"   1½"

On the bottom chord, mark the
length of the three top chords:
the sloping sections at either
end and the level section in
the middle. ▪

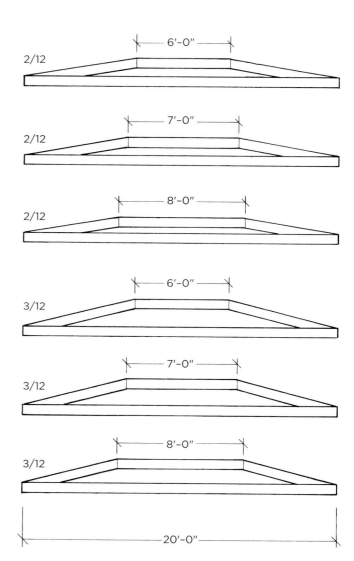

2/12   6'-0"

2/12   7'-0"

2/12   8'-0"

3/12   6'-0"

3/12   7'-0"

3/12   8'-0"

20'-0"

The pitch of the sloped sections
of the top chord and the length
of the level section affect the
profile of the bridge. My design
features a 3-in-12 pitch (3" of rise
for every 12" of run) and an 8'
level section. ▪

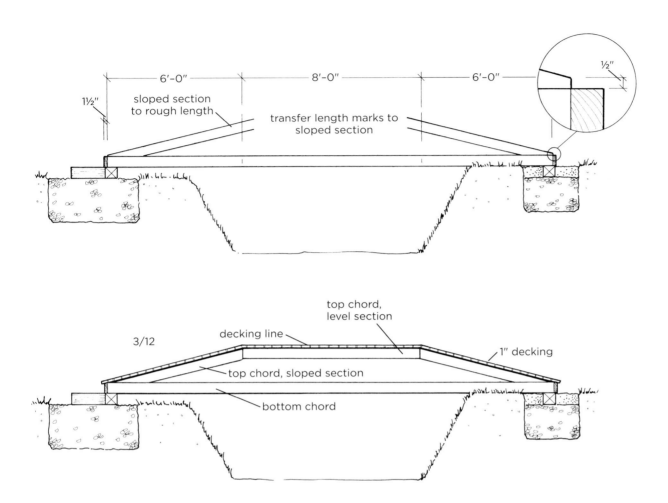

Set your adjustable triangle to the desired pitch (3-in-12 in my design) and, starting just inside the band joists, draw the sloping sections. Draw the lines long. Draw the top chord ½ inch above the band joist so the decking passes above the band joists. Then, with the triangle, mark the length of the level section by extending the marks from the bottom chord. To experiment with a 2-in-12 slope or with center sections of different lengths, do one or more overlays with tissue trace. Draw the level section last.

Next, indicate the thickness of the decking (1 inch in my design), so you'll remember to account for it when determining the height of the top rail. If the decking thickness is unknown at this time, assume 1-inch decking for trusses set 16 inches on center and 2-inch decking for trusses set 24 inches on center. (See page 145 for more on decking thickness.)

Indicate the thickness of the decking on your drawing, so you'll remember to account for it when determining top-rail height. ▪

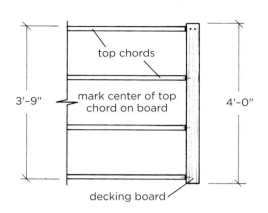

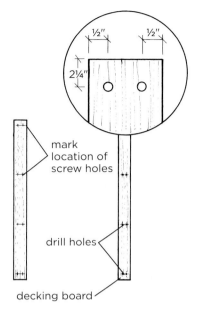

top chords

mark center of top chord on board

3'-9"

4'-0"

decking board

½" ½"

2¼"

mark location of screw holes

drill holes

decking board

Transfer the center lines of the top chords to the decking template, then mark locations of screw holes. Predrill for easy installation.

Preparing the Decking Boards

Measure the width of the frame, add the required amount of overhang at the sides, and cut a board to the correct length (4 feet in this design). Use this board as a template for the remaining decking boards and cut them.

Predrill holes for easy installation. To create a pattern for drilling holes, mark the center of the top chord on the face of a board, being sure to allow for the appropriate overhangs. With a square, draw a line across the face of the board, measure in ½ inch from each edge, and drill and countersink to accept the screws. Use this piece to mark screw locations on the other boards, then drill the holes.

Install the Decking Boards

When all the boards are prepared, treat the undersides of the boards with preservative. It's a quick job to screw the boards into place. Position the first board so it has proper overhangs, then install the screws. Move the second board into position and place spacers between the two boards. Make sure the ends of the second board are properly aligned with the ends of the first board and secure the screws. Leave the top-chord bracing in place until you reach it with the decking. Check frequently to be sure the decking is being installed perpendicular to the frame (see illustration on page 191).

Continue working in this manner until all boards are installed. When you encounter a post, notch the decking around it. Measure the depth and length of the notch and cut it partway through with a power saw; finish the cut with a handsaw. For more decking tips, see page 171.

STRAIGHTEN BOWS

Straighten any bowed decking boards by securing one end, then pulling or prying the problem board tight against the spacer and securing it. Continue working this way until you reach the end of the board.

INSTALL OVER-THE-POST RAILING WITH INTERMEDIATE RAILS

Double-check the posts to be sure they are still plumb. If not, bring them back into alignment.

Hold up a piece of railing stock (2×6 stock in this design) to the posts and mark the length. Mark the middle, level section from the outer edges of the posts. For the two cuts of the level top-rail section to be precisely the same length as those in the sloped sections, they must be cut at an angle equal to half the degree of slope. In this design, we need two 7-degree cuts for a 14-degree, 3-in-12 slope (or two 4.75-degree cuts for a 9.5-degree, 2-in-12 slope). Mark the board as indicated in the illustration, set the saw to 7 degrees, and cut the board. Position the top rail so the ends are flush with the posts and it overhangs each side by 1 inch, then tack it in place.

Next, on a piece of top-rail stock longer than needed for the sloping section, cut a 7-degree angle. Butt this cut against the one on the level section; the fit should be tight. If it's not, trim it and/or the level-section cut until it is. Then cut the rail to length, being sure to allow for the horizontal distance the rail projects beyond the post (10 inches in this design). Do the same for the other sloping rail. Nail both sections in place.

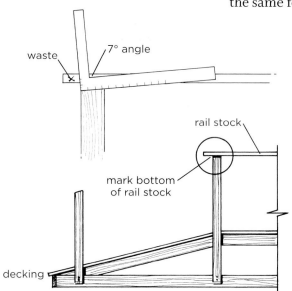

For a 7-degree cut on the level top-rail section, position a framing square at 1½-in-12, as shown, and mark the edge of the top rail. Using the square as a guide, extend the line across the top of the top rail; cut along this line.

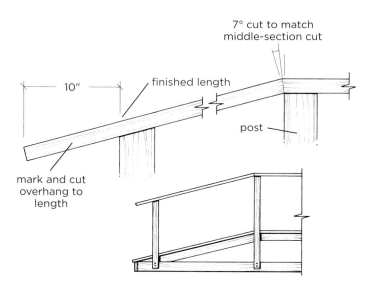

Cut a 7-degree angle on the section of top rail for the sloped section. Butt it up against the middle top rail; the fit should be tight. Mark out the length of the overhang, then cut the rail to length and nail in place.

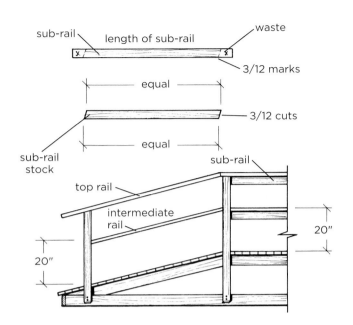

Cut and install the sub-rails and intermediate rails. The top rail protects the end grain of the posts, and the intermediate rail is flush with the outer edges of the posts.

Next, install the sub-rails. The sub-rails at the sloped sections must be cut to match the slope of the bridge. For the most accurate results, hold a section of sub-rail up to the post where it will be installed, then mark top and bottom of the cut. Use a square to scribe the line for the plumb cut. Do the same for the other sub-rails, then cut them. Hold each section of railing in position under the top rail and screw it in place. Also, nail down through the top rail into the sub-rail.

Next, install the intermediate rail and its sub-rail. Measure up from the decking the correct height (20 inches in this design). Then, as before, measure, cut, and install the rails. Remember to cut the sloping sections at the proper angle.

Finishing Touches

Sand and smooth rough edges and surfaces. Pay particular attention to places that might be prone to splintering. If necessary, glue with a water-proof glue or nail them in place before they cause problems or get worse.

Apply a sealer or stain to help protect the bridge from the elements. Choose an environmentally friendly water-based product. You will have to reapply any type of preservative regularly, perhaps yearly, so choose one that is easy to apply.

Two years ago, the view from my lower deck to the north along the west side of the house was an eyesore. The rough path I had carved out about eight years earlier was overgrown with weeds, tree seedlings, and encroaching brush. The sunny, west-facing hillside was in a similarly sorry state, and the bridge site was worse. As I stand here today gazing at the stone wall and up along the stepping-stone path, I'm delighted by the transformation. The careful planning, research, and expert assistance combined to produce a result that met and even exceeded my expectations.

First and foremost, the path, steps, and footbridge closed the circle on our property and connected us with the other side. Strolling around the pond is something we now do regularly.

The seat in the retaining wall is much sought after, particularly in early spring and late fall when the slanting sun warms the stone and those who sit there. The dark, mysterious area beyond the apparent end of the path beckons one to explore. The laurel and hemlock boughs reveal glimpses of the footbridge, urging the walker forward. The partially buried steps with bark-mulch treads blend wonderfully with the hillside, and the bridge has welcomed many visitors who pause to lean on the railing and talk.

One of the most exciting and unforeseen successes of the projects is how they look from inside the house. From the living room window, the seat appears to embrace my favorite oak tree. The plantings beckon the viewer to the window, and from there it's possible to look down the path into the woods and off to the right to see the bridge.

Our once shabby backyard has been transformed into an inviting and relaxing garden that our family thoroughly enjoys. The effort was worth it. I hope you'll feel the same way about your projects.

Cover photographs
© Roger Foley: back cover
Blake Gardner: front cover, bottom right
© Janet Loughrey: front cover, left
© Maggie Oster: front cover, top right

Interior photographs
© R. Todd Davis: xi
© Joseph DeSciose: 3, 5 top, 10 top
© Alan and Linda Detrick Photography/garden design by
    Cording Landscape: 5 bottom
© Roger Foley: ii right, 8 top, 11 right, 15, 20 bottom, 116
Blake Gardner: x, 6 top left and right, 19 right, 22 top, 24, 38, 212, 217,
    219, 221
© Lynn Karlin: 18 bottom
© Rosemary Kautzky: 7 bottom, 9 bottom
© Janet Loughrey: ii bottom left
© J. Paul Moore Photography: 2 bottom, 6 bottom
© Maggie Oster: ii top left, vii, 2 top, 7 top, 8 bottom, 9 top right,
    10 bottom left, 12, 13 bottom, 14 middle left and right, 16 top,
    22 bottom, 23, 70, 141
© Jerry Pavia: xiv, 4, 9 top left, 13 top, 14 bottom left, 17 all, 18 top, 19 left
© Neil Soderstrom: 20 top, 21
© Mark Turner: 10 right, 14 top, 16 bottom

INDEX

Note: Numbers in **boldface** indicate charts; numbers in *italics* indicate photographs.

227

treads, 120, 124, 125, 126, 127

width, 122, **122**

steps, types of

composite, 118, 119

drystone, 123, 129, 139

with earthen treads, 123, 129, 136

helical, 118, 119

with infill treads, 123, 129, 137

one and two-stride, 125, **128**

one-piece, 129, 138

on-grade, 120, 122–23, 124, 125, 126, **128,** 134

stepping-stone, 122–23, 129, 135

straight-run, 118

stone. *See also* flagstone; paths, stepping-stone

choice of, 47–51, **48**

edgings, 90, 91, 104

finish type of, **49,** 49–51

sources of, 47–49

steps with, 17, 123, 135, 138, 139

tools, 43, 51

types of, 47, **48**

uses of, 17

utility type of, **50,** 51

variable names of, **49,** 49–51, **50**

stonemason's hammer, 43

stonework

breaking technique in, 51, 52

cutting technique in, 51, 54–55

nibbling technique in, 51, 52–53

splitting technique in, 51, 54

truing and squaring technique in, 51, 53

structures

primary existing, 33

secondary existing, 33

switchbacks, 84

T

tape measures, 40

templates, 31

3–4-5 method, 36

timber steps, 17

tools, 39

earth work, 41

lifting and moving, 42

for plank footbridges, 152

safety and, 42

stone and masonry, 43, 51

woodworking, 44

topography, 39

paths and, 75, 78

tracing paper, 31

transit, 34, 40

transitions along paths, 82, 83

creation of, 82, 83

railings and, 83

trees

as path canopies, 74

roots of, 112

site plans and, 33

trellis, 74

triangles, 31

T-square, 31

U

utilities, 33

V

vibrating plate compactor, 41

W

walls

cheek, 128

as path edges and borders, 73, 80

water

aesthetics of, 16

conservation of, **46**

footbridges across, 22, 143, 144

joisted footbridges across, 22, 172

plank footbridges across, 20, 148

water fountains, 16

wetlands conservation, 143

wet spots, 20, 33

wheelbarrows, 42

wheeled traffic, 20, 76, 120

wildflowers, *18*

wood

composite lumber, 65

rot-resistant, **63**

sources of, 65–66

treated, 62

types of, 27, 61–65

working with, 167

wood, fibrous

bark mulch, 62

pine needles and leaves, 61

wood chips, 62

wood, solid, 62

boards, 64

poles, logs and rounds, 63

timbers and dimension stock, 64

wood, working with, 61

crosscutting and, 67

hammering and, 66–67

notching and, 68

ripping and, 67

tools for, 44

Y

Y-intersections, 83

Other Storey Titles You Might Enjoy

Deckscaping by Barbara W. Ellis. Transform any deck from an overly exposed flat stretch of space to a cool, private expansion of the house's living area. Trellises, lighting, plantings, and furniture are all covered. 176 pages. Paperback. ISBN 1-58017-408-6.

Designing Your Gardens and Landscapes by Janet Macunovich. This 12-step approach to home landscape design is just the thing for new homeowners or first-time landscapers. Focuses on individual preferences, natural restrictions, and climatic concerns of the landscaper; appropriate for any region. 176 pages. Paperback. ISBN 1-58017-315-2.

Garden Retreats by David and Jeanie Stiles. Garden structure, from simple benches to elegant gazebos, can provide the focal points for relaxing garden retreats; step-by-step instructions for 22 projects. 160 pages. Paperback. ISBN 1-58017-149-4.

Grasses by Nancy Ondra. Ornamental grasses stabilize soil, retard erosion, and conserve water. Complete guide to using ornamental grasses in combination with perennials, annuals, shrubs, and other garden plants. 144 pages. Paperback. ISBN 1-58017-423-X.

Landscaping Makes Cents by Frederic C. Campbell and Richard L. Dube. Practical advice for homeowners who want to add value and beauty to property through careful landscape design. 176 pages. Paperback. ISBN 0-88266-948-6.

Natural Stonescapes by Richard L. Dubé and Frederick C. Campbell. Create beautiful landscapes that mimic the forms of nature with more than 20 designs for stone groupings appropriate for all types of sites. 176 pages. Paperback. ISBN 1-58017-092-7.

Outdoor Water Features by Alan and Gill Bridgewater. Add the sparkle and serenity of water to your landscape with these 16 functional and beautiful projects. 128 pages. Paperback. ISBN 1-58017-334-9.

Shady Retreats by Barbara Ellis. Turn shady nooks into colorful outdoor living spaces with 20 creative plans from a patio adjoining the house to a wooded spot next to the flower garden. 192 pages. Paperback. ISBN 1-58017-472-8.

Stonework by Charles McRaven. Discover the satisfaction of working with stone and learn the tricks of the trade with this collection of projects for garden paths and walls, porches, pools, seats, waterfalls, a bridge, and more. 192 pages. Paperback. ISBN 0-88266-976-1.

These and other books from Storey Publishing are available wherever quality books are sold or by calling 1-800-441-5700. Visit us at www.storey.com.